"Richard Kim's book offers a pithy introduction to how Confucianism contributes to thinking about the good life for us now. I came away convinced that there are universal features of well-being, and also that some things that make a life good depend on one's stage in life, and the particulars of one's culture. Well-written and extremely accessible."

—*Owen Flanagan, Duke University, USA. Author of*
The Geography of Morals: Varieties of Moral Possibility

"At long last, we have a sophisticated and systematic account of early Confucian views on well-being and its relations to ethics. Kim's book is the best on these subjects. He offers a sympathetic and plausible exposition of early Confucianism and makes compelling arguments for an account of well-being that is holistic and developmental, and he paints a very appealing portrait of what he calls 'ethical equanimity', which is one of Confucianism's distinctive contributions to philosophical reflection on well-being and the good life."

—*Justin Tiwald, San Francisco State University, USA*

"Richard Kim's book is a superb introduction to the Confucian conception of human well-being embedded in the thought of Confucius, Mencius, and Xunzi. His advocacy of a Confucian approach to well-being, admirable for its clarity, is informed by his familiarity with the best scholarship on Confucianism, recent empirical research on moral development, and contemporary philosophical theories of prudential value."

—*Richard Kraut, Northwestern University, USA*

"Richard Kim's fascinating and engaging book brings the Confucian tradition into the Western philosophical discussion of well-being in a more sustained and thorough way than any treatment of which I'm aware. Revealing instructive similarities and differences between the traditions, and engaged with the scientific literature as well, this book is a major contribution to the contemporary philosophy of well-being."

—*Daniel Haybron, Saint Louis University, USA*

T0316361

Confucianism and the Philosophy of Well-Being

Well-being is topic of perennial concern. It has been of significant interest to scholars across disciplines, culture, and time. But like morality, conceptions of well-being are deeply shaped and influenced by one's particular social and cultural context. We ought to pursue, therefore, a cross-cultural understanding of well-being and moral psychology by taking seriously reflections from a variety of moral traditions.

This book develops a Confucian account of well-being, considering contemporary accounts of ethics and virtue in light of early Confucian thought and philosophy. Its distinctive approach lies in the integration of Confucian moral philosophy, contemporary empirical psychology, and contemporary philosophical accounts of well-being.

Richard Kim organizes the book around four main areas: the conception of virtues in early Confucianism and the way that they advance both individual and communal well-being; the role of Confucian ritual practices in familial and communal ties; the developmental structure of human life and its culmination in the achievement of sagehood; and the sense of joy that the early Confucians believed was central to the virtuous and happy life.

Richard Kim is Assistant Professor of Philosophy at Loyola University Chicago, USA.

Routledge Focus on Philosophy

Routledge Focus on Philosophy is an exciting and innovative new series, capturing and disseminating some of the best and most exciting new research in philosophy in short book form. Peer reviewed and, at a maximum of fifty thousand words, shorter than the typical research monograph, *Routledge Focus on Philosophy* titles are available in both ebook and print on demand format. Tackling big topics in a digestible format the series opens up important philosophical research for a wider audience, and as such is invaluable reading for the scholar, researcher and student seeking to keep their finger on the pulse of the discipline. The series also reflects the growing interdisciplinarity within philosophy and will be of interest to those in related disciplines across the humanities and social sciences.

For more information about this series, please visit: www.routledge.com/Routledge-Focus-on-Philosophy/book-series/RFP

Confucianism and the Philosophy of Well-Being

Richard Kim

Routledge
Taylor & Francis Group

LONDON AND NEW YORK

First published 2020
by Routledge
4 Park Square, Milton Park, Abingdon, Oxon OX14 4RN
605 Third Avenue, New York, NY 10017

First issued in paperback 2023

Routledge is an imprint of the Taylor & Francis Group, an informa business

British Library Cataloguing-in-Publication Data
A catalogue record for this book is available from the British Library

Library of Congress Cataloging-in-Publication Data
Names: Kim, Richard, author.
Title: Confucianism and the philosophy of well-being / Richard Kim.
Description: Abingdon, Oxon ; New York, NY : Routledge, 2020. | Series:
    Routledge focus on philosophy | Includes bibliographical references and
    index.
Identifiers: LCCN 2019051024 (print) | LCCN 2019051025 (ebook) | ISBN
    9781138037922 (hardback) | ISBN 9781315177601 (ebook)
Subjects: LCSH: Philosophy, Confucian. | Confucianism. | Well-being.
Classification: LCC B127.C65 K5115 2020 (print) | LCC B127.C65 (ebook) |
    DDC 181/.112—dc23
LC record available at https://lccn.loc.gov/2019051024
LC ebook record available at https://lccn.loc.gov/2019051025

ISBN: 978-1-03-257009-9 (pbk)
ISBN: 978-1-138-03792-2 (hbk)
ISBN: 978-1-315-17760-1 (ebk)

DOI: 10.4324/9781315177601

Typeset in Times New Roman
by Apex CoVantage, LLC

Publisher's Note
The publisher has gone to great lengths to ensure the quality of this reprint but
points out that some imperfections in the original copies may be apparent.

Contents

Acknowledgements

Despite its relatively small size, this book took many years to complete. My study of contemporary theories of well-being began while working on my dissertation. Accordingly, I should begin by thanking my wonderful advisor, David Solomon. He was an exemplary advisor: generous, kind, and broad-minded, with a keen eye for spotting what is (and isn't) deep or interesting.

The trajectory of my research was, to my great benefit, reshaped when I took up a postdoctoral research fellowship at the City University of Hong Kong to work with the great PJ Ivanhoe on Korean and comparative philosophy. During these years I studied early Confucianism and Korean Neo-Confucianism, learning much from the wisdom of PJ, who taught me so much of what I know of East Asian philosophy. I am greatly in his debt. I also had the great fortune of meeting many terrific scholars during this period, including Sungmoon Kim, Ruiping Fan, Eirik Harris, Owen Flanagan, Youngsun Back, Hsin-wen Lee, and Wenqing Zhao. I am grateful to all of them for both friendship and intellectual nourishment.

I also met a number of terrific philosophers during my time as a postdoctoral fellow at Saint Louis University for the Happiness and Well-Being Project directed by Dan Haybron, including Jason Chen, Jonathan Reibsamen, and Matt Shea. I owe the greatest debt to Dan, whose outstanding work on happiness and well-being continues to inspire me. He is also one of the kindest, most considerate people I have ever met.

For discussion and written comments for this book, I must thank Steve Angle, Youngsun Back, Anne Baril, Tom Carson, Tim Connolly, Eirik Harris, Dan Haybron, PJ Ivanhoe, Micah Lott, Hui-chieh Loy, Fr. James Dominic Rooney, OP, Justin Tiwald, and Xueying Wang. Their comments saved me from many blunders and dramatically improved the quality of this book. I am truly grateful to all of them. A special thanks also goes to Gina Lebkuecher, who also offered substantive comments and also did excellent work in editing the manuscript.

I am also very grateful to both Adam Johnson and Tony Bruce at Routledge, who displayed great patience as I took many more years to complete this book than I had anticipated.

While working on this book I was generously supported by an Academy of Korean Studies Grant funded by the Korean Government (MEST) (AKS-2011-AAA-2102) and the John Templeton Foundation. The City University of Hong Kong, Saint Louis University, and Loyola University Chicago (where I am currently employed) all provided me with a supportive environment for scholarly work.

Some of the chapters include material that I have published elsewhere, and I thank the publishers for allowing me to reprint that material with modifications. The publications I've incorporated into this book include "Well-Being and Confucianism" in the *Routledge Handbook of Philosophy of Well-Being*, ed. Guy Fletcher (Routledge); "Early Confucianism and Contemporary Moral Psychology," *Philosophy Compass* (2016), https://doi.org/10.1111/phc3.12341; "The Role of Human Nature in Moral Inquiry: MacIntyre, Mencius, and Xunzi," *History of Philosophy Quarterly* 32(4) (2015); "Human Nature and Moral Sprouts: Mencius on the Pollyanna Problem," *Pacific Philosophical Quarterly* 99(1) (2017); "Filial Piety and Business Ethics: A Confucian Reflection" (with Reuben Mondejar and Chris Chu) in *Springer Handbook on Virtue Ethics in Business and Management*, ed. Chris Provis (Springer).

Finally, I thank my wife, Xueying Wang, who has shown me much love and support while writing this book. I dedicate this book to her.

For Xueying

我心屬於你

Introduction

On the first day of my Introduction to Philosophy class, I tell my students that philosophy is the love of wisdom. After all, it's the original meaning of the ancient Greek term from which the word is derived. But to some of us academic philosophers, it sounds a little pompous and disingenuous. Is this *really* what we pursue? Wisdom, after all, is not just truth. It is much grander, fulfilling, and rich. A wicked person might have a lot of knowledge and be dangerously effective in wielding it, but we would be unwilling to call such a person wise. Wisdom seems to imply that one knows how to live well and virtuously, going after what is important in life, with grace, compassion, justice, and all those good qualities we admire.

The Confucians were all about the pursuit of wisdom, of organizing one's life well for oneself, family, community, and ultimately the world. Their primary interests were not in building theories but in living well. They stand as part of a long and venerable movement of those who conceived of philosophy as a *way of life*, as directed toward human fulfillment.[1]

Contemporary Western discussions of welfare are dominated by debates concerning theories of well-being. A variety of philosophical theories, some with ancient roots, have developed over the years with increasing sophistication. This literature is already vast and continues to grow. But philosophers have begun voicing dissatisfaction with these debates, due to their seemingly interminable quality and lack of clear progress. Simon Keller describes the current state of play:

> Philosophers have put a great deal of effort into constructing theories of welfare, but the enterprise is not in good shape. Each of the three standard theories of welfare—the mental state theory, the desire theory, and the objective list theory—seems subject to devastating objections. There have been attempts to go beyond the standard theories and attempts to build theories that straddle the boundaries between them, but none has established itself as a popular alternative.
>
> (Keller 2009: 656)

And Michael Bishop writes:

> The product of the traditional approach to the study of well-being has been rampant theoretical dissensus. Peruse the philosophical literature on well-being and you will find a diverse smorgasbord of theories from which you can select that best fits your commonsense judgments. Profound disagreement is not a temporary aberration that will resolve itself with more time and study. It is the entirely predictable result of an approach to philosophy that tells us to build theories that capture our commonsense judgments despite the fact that we have no consensus about those judgments. Even so, the traditional approach dominates the philosophical landscape. It has not had enough success to deserve the hegemony it currently enjoys.
>
> (Bishop 2015: 32–33)

I believe that there are at least two reasons for this lack of progress in philosophical theorizing about well-being:

> *Complexity*: Human lives are enormously complex, requiring a wide assortment of goods at different stages of life. The differences during infancy, childhood, and adulthood are dramatic in terms of physical, emotional, and intellectual needs as well as both physical and social dependency.
>
> *Entanglement*: Well-being, at the substantive level, is closely intertwined with other values such as moral or aesthetic value.

The first point is also connected to a thesis that the kind of well-being that really matters pertains to one's life as a whole.[2] In other words, how much prudential value an activity or experience carries depends on its contribution to the overall prudential value of one's life. But figuring out whether certain experiences, activities, or events are good or bad for someone from this broad perspective is extremely difficult, and it is hard to see how a single theory could explain every instance of prudential value or disvalue.[3]

The second thesis is more controversial. Philosophers working on developing a theory of well-being often sharply distinguish well-being from other domains of value in order to uncover well-being's true nature considered apart from other kinds of concern that mark human life (e.g. morality or virtue). We want to know what *well-being* is, just in itself, without factoring in moral (or other value) considerations. But while well-being and other values such as virtue or beauty are conceptually distinct, our thoughts about well-being tend to draw on other values.[4] Further, there is unfortunately no consensus about the kinds of values or goods that are constitutive of well-being. Are values like knowledge, friendships, or moral virtue fundamentally (or non-instrumentally) good for us? There remains rampant disagreement.[5]

Driven in part by the worry that the study of well-being has become too abstract and theory driven, some contemporary philosophers have sought to advance our understanding of well-being through a more empirically grounded approach, which integrates philosophical discussions of well-being with research in psychology and cognitive science.[6] On this view, we cannot advance in our ethical understanding unless we pay careful attention to the realities of human cognition, emotion, and motivation from a range of perspectives.

Taking up the spirit of this broader movement toward a more contextualized, psychologically and culturally grounded inquiry into well-being, this book focuses on a single moral tradition, Confucianism—or early Confucianism, to be more precise—which powerfully influenced the moral and cultural values of East Asian societies. (I will say more about the historical and cultural context of Confucianism later.) I draw on the thoughts contained in three core texts from the early Confucian tradition: the *Analects*, the *Mengzi*, and the *Xunzi*. I believe these three texts offer enough material to extract a core account of well-being as represented in the early Confucian tradition.[7] One of the advantages of reflecting on well-being from the perspective of a wide-ranging, well-developed tradition like Confucianism is that it provides a picture of whole human lives, integrating a wide range of values and concerns, providing some unity and structure to the variety of human experiences relevant to well-being.

Reflections on a historically significant moral tradition like Confucianism also helps us see that ethical thought finds its roots in the real lives of flesh and blood humans as they struggle to realize meaning and goodness in their lives. Moral concepts, especially those that have a foothold in lived human experience, do not arise in a vacuum but develop within societies, cultures, and traditions. While it is sometimes appropriate to regiment concepts to play specialized roles, concepts like justice, goodness, virtue—as well as happiness and well-being—have content that has undoubtedly been deeply influenced by ordinary discourse. This is one reason concepts like happiness or well-being are employed by the general population and by scholars across different disciplines in a variety of ways. Such concepts are messy, and one of the tasks of philosophers is to help clarify and make sense of them.

A full-blown inquiry into the topic of well-being requires not only ground-level work on concept clarification but also the integration of knowledge from a variety of disciplines: cultural and religious studies, literature, anthropology, sociology, psychology, cognitive science, and other domains of study relevant to the quality of human lives. This is a hard task, especially given how specialized disciplines have become. Nevertheless, this sort of interdisciplinary study offers the best shot at moving forward our understanding of human flourishing. By triangulating across different areas of study, we can check and verify truth claims with greater warrant; because these different fields of inquiry employ their own distinctive methodologies and tools, they can help us correct or account for blind spots in other domains. I will take up this interdisciplinary approach by integrating discussions from a range of different fields when I believe they help support or enrich philosophical discussions.

If concepts like happiness or well-being arise within the ethical frameworks of particular traditions, cultures, and societies, then we ought to study how such concepts are employed in other cultures and learn from varied conceptions of well-being. Deeply reflecting on cultures that are different from our own can help us take on new perspectives and uncover different models of flourishing. As Alasdair MacIntyre remarks, this is especially important for moral philosophizing:

> [T]he study of moral philosophy has become divorced from the study of morality or rather of moralities and by so doing has distanced itself from practice. We do not expect serious work in the philosophy of physics from students who have never studied physics or on the philosophy of law from students who have never studied law. But there is not even a hint of suggestion that courses in social and cultural anthropology and in certain areas of sociology and psychology should be a prerequisite for graduate work in moral philosophy. . . . Yet without such courses no adequate sense of the varieties of moral possibility can be acquired. One remains imprisoned by one's upbringing.[8]

The suggestion is that moral philosophers should not detach themselves from reflecting on the concrete, local, and culturally embodied morality that influences the lives of ordinary people.

Similarly, reflections on the good life by important thinkers from a variety of moral traditions also provide substantial material for thinking about happiness and well-being. Deepening our understanding of how different thinkers from a variety of different cultures and philosophical traditions conceived of well-being may open up new lines of thought about human flourishing and draw attention to sources of well-being that deserve more attention. Such studies are necessary not only for extending our understanding of human flourishing but also for moving us to critically examine our own basic assumptions underlying our thoughts about well-being, thus revealing ways in which our accounts of well-being may be rooted in local cultural values.

The Confucian tradition takes well-being and morality as closely bound together, and its approach to ethical concerns take a different direction when compared to certain modern approaches to morality. Elaborating on the second point, modern philosophers, especially Kantians and consequentialists, tend to take the core of morality as constituted by the impartial duties we have toward all rational beings (or perhaps all sentient creatures), independent of their relationships to us. It is only after we establish the nature and role of impartial obligations toward all that we should investigate the nature and content of particular obligations we may have toward those we bear a special connection to. We may think of this as an *outside-in* approach: we begin by looking at our obligations toward all people (or perhaps all subjects of welfare), and then gradually narrow our focus toward those we care more about.[9] The Confucian view, on the other hand, takes an *inside-out* approach. The core of morality lies in those local, particular relationships that begin within the family and community; it is only after we understand the nature and role of special relationships, and the obligations arising from them, that we should start reflecting on questions about the obligations we have toward everybody else. Consider the following passage from the *Mengzi*:

> Mengzi said, "Gentlemen, in relation to animals, are sparing of them, but are not benevolent toward them. In relation to the people, they are benevolent toward them, but do not treat them as kin. They treat their kin as kin, but then are benevolent toward the people. They are benevolent toward the people, and then are sparing of animals."
>
> (*Mengzi* 7A45)[10]

The idea represented in this passage, well-known to scholars of Confucian thought as "graded" or "differentiated" love, is a significant part of the Confucian moral tradition and will be explored at greater length in the course of this work.

Besides the three classical Confucian texts I focus on (*Analects, Mengzi*, and *Xunzi*), there are other classical texts in both early and later Confucianism that are interesting and important. But given that these texts alone have generated over 2,000 years of extensive commentaries, our hands will already be full.[11] It is also worth noting, as scholars would rightly point out, that the ideas or arguments within these three texts are not always in conformity and that there are substantive differences among the three thinkers represented in these texts. Still, I think these three texts together provide a coherent and powerful ethical tradition that is worth careful examination.[12]

Finally, the organizing principle of this book—one that has deeply influenced my choice of sources to reference—is contemporary philosophical relevance. This is the principle driving my discussions of research from other disciplines such as social psychology, and so I do not focus on the Sinological or historical issues a much larger book would do well to include. In this book I will only be able to give a brief picture of Confucianism's intellectual and historical background. But it is important to note that one engaging in the history of philosophy should not fail to take seriously the linguistic, intellectual, and cultural background of the philosophers one is learning from. By detaching historical thinkers from their intellectual and cultural context, we risk engaging in a barren enterprise. But if we are to ever bring some part of the history of philosophy to productively engage with contemporary issues, we need to start thinking seriously about their ideas and how they relate to topics that interest us today. Doing this well requires knowledge of the intellectual background that gave those historical discussions their sense and purpose.[13]

If we simply wrench ideas or arguments from their historical context, thinking that doing so allows us to evaluate them according to their "pure" philosophical merits, we risk distorting those ideas and arguments and can easily miss out on what gives them their significance within a particular conversation or tradition. After all, for those of us who think these historical thinkers and their arguments matter to us today, we are operating with the assumption that *their* ideas and arguments still have something to contribute to our ongoing discussions; we need to get clear on what they were claiming and why it mattered to them.[14]

In the course of our reflections on the Confucian tradition, three central points will emerge that I take as bearing the most significant connections to our contemporary understanding of well-being:

1   *Well-being holism*: Well-being is inseparable from other fundamental values, most importantly virtue or moral goodness. This is contrary to the dominant view among Western contemporary philosophers that well-being is independent of moral considerations. As we think hard about the Confucian conception of well-being, we will explore why our understanding of well-being cannot be detached from other normative values (especially virtue) in this way. We will examine one account of well-being and morality that understands the two as inextricably bound together.

2   *Relationality thesis*: Human relationships lie at the heart of well-being, and we cannot separate our study of human well-being from an inquiry

into what builds and sustains good families and communities. Our lives gain their sense and meaning through the relationships we build and sustain. We are, in this way, *relational* and *political* animals who live and develop in communication with others. The Confucian tradition takes well-being as only achievable within a particular kind of social life. Well-being takes root in families and communities.

3   *Well-being contextualism*: Human beings are subject to a barrage of external influences that often operate unconsciously. These everyday effects accumulate over time and deeply influence our levels of well-being. Given our sensitivity to situational conditions, human welfare cannot be separated from the sorts of physical, cultural, and social environments that promote flourishing.

As noted earlier, the primary aim of the early Confucians was to improve the quality of lives for themselves and those within their communities. And given the undoubtedly different form of life, entrenched in different values, norms, and practices that framed the culture of this period, their account of well-being will obviously diverge from the accounts of well-being offered by contemporary American philosophers.

These points about cultural influence and context notwithstanding, following the earlier work of Martha Nussbaum we might admit of certain spheres of human experience that are generalizable across cultures due to our shared humanity (Nussbaum 1993). For while different individuals, families, and societies forge different values and paths through life, there are certain physical and psychological parameters that limit what is practically possible for human beings. This is why we can understand the feelings of shame, honor, and loyalty represented in a Kurosawa movie, become moved by the struggles of romantic love in Bollywood films, or feel satisfaction from seeing Sonny Corleone punish his abusive brother-in-law in *The Godfather*. Such movies, and almost every literary classic across cultures, are built on powerful, universal themes of human struggle, emotion, and joy.

Contemporary sociologists and psychologists have also suggested that there are certain foundational values and innate human needs that give substantive shape and structure to human lives and communities. (We will explore these theories later on.) If these theories hold, it seems quite plausible that at least some of the moral foundations or innate human needs are grounded in basic facts about human beings shared across cultures. I contend that the early Confucian moral tradition offers intelligible ways of giving expression to many of these foundational values or needs, drawing our attention to possible goods that might be neglected within our own culture and philosophical inquiries, thereby helping us better understand varieties of human well-being. We will also explore how contemporary theories of psychology offer support to the various values and practices central to the Confucian conception of the good life.

There is a thought common enough among modern intellectuals, and probably ordinary citizens, that ancient texts and the so-called "wisdom of the ages" have little benefit to confer given our extensive and rapidly increasing scientific and medical knowledge. But as Sebastian Junger comments,

> Numerous cross-cultural studies have shown that modern society— despite its nearly miraculous advances in medicine, science, and technology—is afflicted with some of the highest rates of depression, schizophrenia, poor health, anxiety, and chronic loneliness in human history. As affluence and urbanization rise in a society, rates of depression and suicide tend to go *up* rather than down. Rather than buffering people from clinical depression, increased wealth in a society seems to foster it.
>
> (Junger 2016: 18–19)[15]

The idea that modernization and scientific progress proceed hand in hand with human welfare might seem obvious, but it may not be true. This might be due in part to the fact that there appears to be a mismatch between our tribal nature, which was naturally fitted for life in very small communities, and life in the large-scale globalized world in which we find ourselves.[16] Perhaps we are really suited for lives that center on small, close relationships with those that share significant common ideals and pursuits. We have reason to believe that it is those attitudes, dispositions, and traits that help develop and sustain intimate relationships within families and small communities that are most important for human flourishing. While the ills of malnutrition and disease may be gradually eradicated through marvelous developments in modern medicine, there can remain maladies of the soul for which there are no easy remedies: depression, loneliness, and alienation. The central virtues and practices of Confucianism—ritual, deferential respect, filial piety—are particular ways of giving expression to and satisfying our need to belong to a community and share in a life directed toward the common good.

Brief historical background to Confucianism

Before turning to our discussion of contemporary theories of well-being, it will be helpful to provide a brief historical and intellectual background of the Confucian tradition. Confucianism is an ethical tradition with ancient roots spanning 2,500 years of human civilization. To this day it remains a living tradition, continuing to influence the habits, thoughts, and values of cultures and societies throughout the East. Its origin traces back to the teachings of Confucius or "Master Kong" (孔子, 551–479 BCE) who offered a profound ethical vision of the ideal society characterized by peaceful order and humane relationships. The achievement of such a society, Confucius insisted, rested on following "the Way" (*dao* 道)—the correct path of moral transformation—through active participation in rituals or rites (*li* 禮) and the fulfillment of social roles within the context of the family and community.

Born in the ancient state of Lu (what is now China's Shandong province), Confucius lived during a turbulent time marked by political strife. He believed the cause of this decline in the social and political situation of his age was the loss of values and norms central to good families and societies. Confucius understood his task as largely one of recovery: by restoring these cultural values, society would flourish again. As Confucius remarks: "I transmit rather than innovate. I trust in and love the ancient ways" (*Analects* 7.1).[17] Such statements might give the impression of Confucius as a simplistic traditionalist, but, as is evident from other passages, Confucius was willing to revise traditional practice if there was good reason to do so and the original point of the practice did not become distorted (*Analects* 9.3). Nevertheless, Confucius believed that reclaiming past values would help retrieve the peace and stability that had been lost, and in this way some might see him as a romanticizer of the past. But if these forgotten values of the past are critical for fashioning good lives and promoting the common good, Confucius shouldn't be criticized as a mere lover of the past but recognized as someone aiming to restore values that would promote human flourishing. The underlying rationale for taking seriously the principles and values inherent in long-standing traditions is captured by Will and Ariel Durant:

> Out of every hundred new ideas ninety-nine or more will probably be inferior to the traditional responses which they propose to replace. No one man, however brilliant or well-informed, can come in one lifetime of such fullness of understanding as to safely judge and dismiss the customs or instructions of his society, for these are the wisdom of generations after centuries of experiment in the laboratory of history.
>
> (Durant 1968: 34)

Over time rituals and practical rules develop to satisfy the basic human needs, and while they themselves need to be continuously subjected to critical examination, there is often much more practical value in them than initial appearances might suggest. The early Confucian Xunzi (310–235 BCE) believed that the Confucian rituals were the products of sages, developed through a slow process of trial and error, and so could be trusted to reliably guide our lives and society.[18]

The ideas of Confucius we explore are contained in what is now called the *Analects*, a compilation of stories and teachings centered on Confucius and his disciples. While scholarly disputes continue about who exactly composed which parts of the *Analects* and when the composition happened, the text as a whole offers a fairly unified vision of the good life as revealed through the snapshots of Confucius's interactions with students (Schwartz 1985: Chapter 3).

It is worth noting that scholars dispute the legitimacy of the term 'Confucianism' for several reasons. The first is that the sources of the intellectual tradition we label as Confucianism stretches back further than Confucius's *Analects*. Another reason is that the very English term 'Confucianism' seems to date back to the mid-19th century and is thought by some to be highly misleading.[19] For these reasons, many scholars use the traditional Chinese term "rujia" (儒家)—literally, the erudite school—to designate the tradition that we refer to as 'Confucianism.' This is in some ways more accurate and does not give the misleading impression that the tradition began unambiguously with Confucius. On the other hand, as long as we understand these historical points, I don't think we need to jettison the term 'Confucianism.' And even if it is true that Jesuit missionaries came up with this English label long after the establishment of the tradition, what is more important is that there was a recognizable intellectual tradition centered on the core ideas of Confucius that staked out a distinctive line of thought.

The two major early Confucians that we focus on in this book, Mencius (or Mengzi) and Xunzi, can be understood as taking up the teachings of Confucius and extending them by grounding them in more reflective accounts of human nature and moral psychology. While there are scholarly disagreements about the extent to which Mencius and Xunzi share a single Confucian vision of the good life, there is no doubt that they share key points of agreement that mark their position as properly Confucian. Both thinkers, for example, accept certain key virtues as foundational to living well including benevolence (*ren* 仁), righteousness (*yi* 義), ritual propriety (*li* 禮), practical wisdom (*zhi* 智), and filial piety (*xiao* 孝). (We will explore these virtues and other Confucian values later.) They also accept a key Confucian idea, which I will call the *primacy of cultivation*, which sees individual ethical perfection as having practical priority over issues about law or political structure. Rather than emphasizing the use of laws and punishment, the Confucians believed peace and good order required real transformation from the ground up. On this view, it is necessary that the people and most importantly, the ruler (or persons in positions of power), develop good character. This is not to say that the Confucians were staunchly opposed to laws of any kind, but that they did not think they could be counted on as the proper basis for a flourishing society:

> The Master said, "If you try to guide the common good with coercive regulations (*zheng* 政) and keep them in line with punishments, the common people will become evasive and will have no sense of shame. If, however, you guide them with Virtue, and keep them in line by means of ritual, the people will have a sense of shame and will rectify themselves."
>
> (*Analects* 2.3)

The underlying thought here seems to be that the virtues provide a much more solid foundation for a healthy society than law alone would, by fostering deep and meaningful human relationships built on mutually shared affection and trust. If people were to form such relationships, the chance of bad human acts and social disorder would be significantly diminished.

The idea behind the primacy of cultivation is not to claim that personal self-cultivation is the final end of Confucianism, but that from a practical point of view the most important end—a flourishing society—can be achieved if and only if individuals develop the Confucian virtues.[20] In this way, Confucian ethics bears a strong connection to Confucian political philosophy because ethical reflection cannot be detached from political reflection about what would be best for the society as a whole.[21] Underlying this strong connection between ethics and politics is also the Confucian view of the self as substantially constituted by significant relationships and an account of well-being that sees individual flourishing as inseparable from the flourishing of others (at least those that become central to one's own life).

It is important to note again that Confucianism, with its long, complex history, is not a monolithic system of ideas but has undergone a variety of revisions and transformations, directed by a long list of luminous minds. One significant development is the movement generally known as Neo-Confucianism, advanced by a list of important thinkers in China, Korea, and Japan including the Cheng Brothers, Zhu Xi, Wang Yangming, Itō Jinsai, Dai Zhen, and Dasan.[22] And Neo-Confucianism, in the hands of these thinkers as well as others, itself took on different forms, absorbing in different ways the influences of other philosophical and religious traditions such as Daoism and Buddhism. As others have remarked, there is no single Confucianism but a variety of *Confucianisms*, each with its distinct set of geographical, cultural, ethical, and metaphysical foundations.

While there is a woeful lack of discussions by or about women within the Confucian tradition, there have nevertheless been important women who have made substantial marks on its history.[23] It is true, however, that Confucianism, at least in the minds of most followers, was generally conceived as an ethics for men. (A notable exception is Li Zhi.)[24] But while we should bemoan the lack of female voices within the Confucian tradition, what we find in the early Confucian and Neo-Confucian texts is the general absence of discussion of women rather than pervasive downgrading of their rational or moral capacities that we often find in classical Western treatises.[25] And while a much lengthier discussion is necessary, the core ideas of Confucianism, in my view, are not gender specific—a position defended by some of the most revered female intellectuals of Korean Neo-Confucianism.[26] These are challenging and complicated issues that deserve more careful discussion, but there are reasons to believe that the patriarchal, sexist attitudes held by Confucian practitioners are not essential to Confucianism as a tradition.[27]

The role and influence of Confucianism in the present day is a topic that is far more complicated than is possible to address adequately here. There is currently a "Confucian revival" promoted by certain governments such as China or Singapore, but there are some complicated questions about the extent to which such revivals are politically driven, cherry-picking ideas that only promote state authority. What seems clear is that whatever one's particular attitudes might be toward Confucianism, its values and ideals are well entrenched within the cultures and societies of East Asia. (As are the values of other traditions such as Daoism and Buddhism.) Of course, whether such values or ideas are *worth* sustaining is a separate philosophical question that cannot be settled through sociological investigation alone.

We find in Confucianism a strong inclination to respect tradition and ancient ways that can seem antithetical to the progressive outlook that most scholars find fitting for modern society. But it is only through struggle and contention that human thought becomes stronger and more refined. We need to learn how to both preserve what is good and valuable through restraint while at the same time maintaining the kind of intellectual humility and open-mindedness that allows for positive revisions and further progress. Drawing on a memorable phrase in the *Analects*, we need to be able to "keep warm the old while understanding the new"[28] (*Analects* 2.11).

Notes

1   They were also interested in truth as well, although their central preoccupation was with the realm of the practical. See Hadot (1995).
2   The strongest version of this thesis is held by Ben Bramble 2018, who argues that only lifetime well-being (rather than momentary or periodic well-being) is intrinsically normatively significant. Bramble even argues that momentary or periodic well-being doesn't exist at all. While I'm not committed to the

non-existence thesis, I find the thesis that it is lifetime well-being that is most normatively significant quite plausible.

3 Of course hedonists or desire-fulfillment theorists will disagree, and I will not pretend to have provided any knockdown arguments against their views here.

4 There are recent studies that argue that even at the conceptual level, the ordinary concept of happiness is intimately tied to moral value. See Phillips *et al.* (2017) and Phillips *et al.* (2014).

5 For example, hedonists would deny that any of these items are fundamentally or basically good for us. And while friendship or some related notion appears on most objective lists of theories, many exclude knowledge or moral virtue from their lists. See Fletcher (2016: 149).

6 See Haybron (2008), Besser-Jones (2014), Bishop (2015), and Alexandrova (2017), and Tiberius (2018).

7 In taking this approach, I do not mean to suggest that there are not real differences (in both content and emphasis) or even conflicts across these texts. Xunzi certainly has historically been read as more outside of the mainstream Confucian tradition, although modern scholars tend to reject this perspective. What I do affirm is that we do find a substantial, coherent account of well-being shared by all three texts. The vision of the sage that we find across these texts seem quite similar. I thank Youngsun Back and Philip Ivanhoe for helping me clarify this point.

8 MacIntyre (2013: 31).

9 We also find this kind of ethical framework in the Mohists, an important and influential early Chinese tradition. See Fraser (2016) for a book-length treatment.

10 Unless noted otherwise, the passages from the *Mengzi* are from Bryan W. Van Norden, trans., *Mengzi: With Selections from Traditional Commentaries* (Indianapolis: Hackett, 2008).

11 Slingerland (2003) and Van Norden (2008) both illuminate classical Chinese texts with the use of significant commentaries.
Outside of these Chinese resources, I will mainly draw on important scholarship of the early Confucian tradition from the English-speaking world, because one of my central aims is to connect the Confucian account of well-being to contemporary Western philosophical discussions. This is not to deny the valuable scholarship produced by the non-English-speaking world.

12 It is also worth noting that we can discuss the core ideas of Buddhism or Aristotelianism as a particular tradition, even though there are always substantial disagreements within each tradition across both thinkers and texts.

13 Doing all of this is a monumental task, and so what is probably needed is a division of intellectual labor. See Linda Zagzebski's discussion of this in Zagzebski (2017: Ch. 7).

14 To address this worry, the discussions in this book will be heavily informed by the works of scholars such as Wm. Theodore de Bary (Bary 1996), A. C. Graham (Graham 1989), Benjamin Schwartz (Schwartz 1985), and David Nivison (Nivison and Van Norden 1996), who have done much to illuminate the cultural and intellectual context within which Confucianism gained its philosophical significance. My debt to these scholars is enormous, but I have relegated their discussions mostly to footnotes for the sake of keeping our eye on philosophical issues.

15 See also Colla *et al.* (2006), Hidaka (2012), Kastrup (2011).

16 For an exploration of this point from a Buddhist perspective, see Wright (2017).

17 Unless noted otherwise, the passages from the *Analects* are given from Edward Slingerland, trans., *Confucius: Analects* (Indianapolis: Hackett, 2003).

18 See Nivison (1996) for a discussion of how Xunzi believed the rituals were the product of sages that took place over a lengthy period of time.

19 Lionel Jensen has argued that the term 'Confucianism' was manufactured by Jesuit missionaries, although Jensen dates the existence of the English term back to 1862 (Jensen 1997: 4). Nicholas Standaert, however, provides some strong arguments against this view in Standaert (1999). As Standaert argues, while the term 'Confucius' can be traced back to the Latinization of *Kongfuzi* by 17th-century Jesuits, the term 'Confucianism' isn't a term we find in the writings of Jesuits.

20 It is not entirely clear exactly who (or how many) must cultivate the virtues for a flourishing society. Some commoners, for example, may simply never be able to fully understand the true meaning of rituals, according to Xunzi. I thank Eirik Harris for this point.

21 For an illuminating treatment of Confucian political philosophy, see Sungmoon Kim, *Democracy in East Asia*.

22 See Graham (1992) and Ivanhoe (2016).

23 See *Collected Life Stories of Women* or *Lienu Zhuan*, usually attributed by scholars to the Han scholar Liu Xiang (c. 79–78 BCE). For a translation, see Kinney (2014). This text and the representation in early China is explored in depth in Raphals (1998). A central claim of Raphals is that women exerted much more influence in early China than is often assumed. Another important source of learning about female Confucian scholars is *The Confucian Four Books for Women: A New Translation of the Nu Sishu and the Commentary of Wang Xiang*. See Pang-White (2018) for an English translation and analysis.

24 See Handler-Spitz et al. (2016). See also Lee (2000, 2013) for a study of Li Zhi.

25 Perhaps the most sexist comment we find in early Confucianism appears in the following passage in the *Mencius*: "The father teaches sons the way of good men; the mother teaches daughters about marriage. [When the mother] sends her daughter to the wedding, she would say 'After getting married, you must be respectful and diligent, and do not go against your husband's will. Women's way is to obey'" (*Mengzi* 3B.2). But even this passage, as Chengyang Li points out, seems more of a descriptive statement centered on the cultural norm.

26 For discussion see Youngmin Kim (2011) and Sungmoon Kim (2014).

27 For detailed studies of this issue, see Raphals (1998), Li (2000), Rosenlee (2006), and Pang-White (2018).

28 Adapted from the original Chinese: 子曰：“溫故而知新，可以為師矣” which may be translated as, "The Master said, 'Someone who keeps warm the old and understands the new—this person can be considered a teacher.'"

1 Concept, theory, and framework

If we are to investigate the early Confucian account of well-being, we need to begin by clarifying what we mean by the term 'well-being.' This is especially important because well-being has been used by philosophers in a variety of ways, and furthermore, it is not clear that there is any specific Chinese character or concept that corresponds to this term.[1] This chapter seeks to clarify the concept of well-being and some related notions and to establish well-being as a framework for understanding the values and practices of the early Confucian tradition. While there remain significant challenges for understanding the concept of well-being, some contemporary conceptual distinctions have advanced our studies. By introducing these distinctions, I hope that we will gain a better grasp of what the early Confucian account of well-being is an account *of*. We will also see the early Confucian thinkers as challenging the way contemporary philosophers separate virtues from well-being by distinguishing well-being from the good life. After clarifying the concept of well-being, I will discuss how the Confucian account of well-being is connected to the various contemporary theories of well-being that have developed in recent years. Finally, I will argue that the concept of well-being can provide a way of organizing the ethical thoughts of early Confucians by providing a structure and aim to their ideas, making their philosophical views clearer and more attractive.

It is worth addressing a more general objection to reflecting on the Confucian account of well-being, which is that 'well-being' and its cognates are English terms and that applying them to the Confucian tradition requires imposing an alien concept that does not really fit and may distort the original Chinese views. This is an instance of a more general worry about connecting historical thinkers to contemporary problems and about carrying out comparative work with thinkers from radically different traditions. While the worry is legitimate, whether it is applicable ought to be judged on a case-by-case basis.[2] There probably are concepts so culturally embedded and unique that these kinds of cross-cultural or cross-historical connections may not help us further develop our own moral understanding.

But while this is a real possibility, there are a variety of concepts and ideas shared across cultures connected to contemporary inquiries. The following question might be helpful: is there a recognizable phenomenon of lives that are flourishing or going well that we find discussed in the Confucian texts? I think the answer is a resounding yes.

Recent philosophers working on well-being have distinguished between thinking about the well-being of individuals at a particular moment in time on the one hand and thinking about well-being of individuals considering their life as a whole on the other. Following Ben Bramble's recent work, we might dub the first notion 'temporal well-being' and the latter 'lifetime well-being.' Later in this book (especially in Chapter 5), I will explain why the Confucians understood lifetime well-being as the more important and fundamental notion. As we will see, the different goods constitutive of the Confucian account of well-being are realized at different stages of one's life, and those activities and qualities that play a pivotal role in this realization can only be developed in the course of a complete life. For example, while filial piety—a central Confucian good—can be practiced as a young child, it is fully expressed as an adult by attending to the needs of one's aging parents and properly mourning after their passing.

Probing the Confucian account of well-being might even challenge the very aim of finding a single theory that can capture the complexities of necessary goods within a human life. On the Confucian view, the human self is substantially constituted by the fundamental roles we occupy in the course of a complete life (e.g. daughter, son, parent, wife, husband, grandparent, teacher, or friend). Different roles will require different goods to flourish within that capacity. (I return to this point in Chapter 4.) From this perspective, given the rich diversity of roles and how they are indexed to radically different stages of human life, it is hard to see how a single theory can completely capture what it is to do well during different various stretches of one's life. Moreover, reflecting again on filial piety, there are times when, on the Confucian view, one ought to grieve and be displeased about some event in one's life, most clearly when one's parent has died. From the Confucian perspective, such grief is ineliminable from human life given that we are creatures of affection and love, so certain negative emotions must be properly expressed through Confucian rituals, rather than eliminated, even though they may contribute to a reduction of temporal or momentary well-being.

The concept of well-being

A cluster of concepts is typically employed to help clarify the concept of well-being, such as the notions of 'happiness,' 'self-interest,' 'good for,' 'good life,' and 'flourishing.' Unfortunately, just how these various concepts—themselves often in need of elucidation—are linked to each other is a difficult issue requiring its own separate treatment. We can perhaps begin by noting broader and narrower senses of 'well-being' that admit of thicker and thinner specifications.

In the thickest sense, well-being is taken as referring to a range of external goods such as wealth, reputation, power, and comfort. Here the term *li* (利) or 'profit' seems closest to this sense.[3] In fact, the early Confucians often attached this narrow sense of well-being to the term *li*, which I will translate as 'profit' in line with the standard translation. The beginning of the *Mengzi* begins with the text's namesake chastising the king for being preoccupied with profit rather than virtues such as righteousness. This distinction between what profits oneself and what virtue requires might seem to already indicate that for Mencius, virtue and one's interests are clearly distinct and potentially in conflict. But here and in other passages we will examine, profit seems narrowly construed as material goods or certain significant external goods such as power or reputation, and so should be distinguished from the more formal, broader concept of well-being. Xunzi also uses the term 'profit' to mark out the concept of material or external goods, although we can see that he also recognizes a different notion of overall benefit distinct from a narrower concept of profit:

> He comes to the point where he loves it [virtue or goodness], and then his eyes love it more than the five colors, his ears love it more than the five tones, his mouth loves it more than the five flavors, and his heart considers it more *profitable* than possessing the whole world. For this reason, power and *profit* cannot sway him, the masses cannot shift him, and nothing in the world can shake him.
>
> (Xunzi, Ch. 1: 8)[4]

Xunzi shifts here between two senses of profit (*li* 利). The first is a broader sense which allows him to claim that the virtuous person (or the person on the road to virtue) takes the path of virtue as more "profitable than possessing the whole world." In other words, the virtuous person sees virtue as more advantageous than goods such as wealth or power. But Xunzi also recognizes a sense of *li* (profit) that is constituted by material goods such as wealth. In ordinary talk and even in academic English discourse, we can find both senses of 'well-being' or 'welfare' at work.

It is important, then, to make sure that the *concept* of well-being is not simply equated with any particular *conception* (or account) of well-being such as health, wealth, or subjective satisfaction.[5] But in a variety of disciplines, this is precisely how the term 'well-being' appears to be used.

In psychology, for example, well-being is often equated with subjective or psychological well-being, what philosophers nowadays tend to call 'happiness.' In economics, well-being is usually equated with preference satisfaction or desire-fulfillment. But whether the best account of well-being is psychological happiness or desire-fulfillment is a deeply contentious matter that cannot be settled through fiat. In fact, the Confucian account of well-being developed in this book will be in conflict with such accounts by taking virtues and certain objectively worthwhile activities (as identified by the early Confucians) as constitutive of well-being.[6]

Well-being is a large, complex, and unwieldy topic, and asking a question like what makes someone's life go well on the whole, all things considered, may just be too complex to answer. As Alexandrova (2017) has recently suggested, it may be more fruitful to focus on specific areas of well-being such as child or elderly well-being and make headway through a more fine-grained, piecemeal process. By circumscribing our reflections on well-being to a specific context such as child well-being, we can also draw on the wealth of empirical research that has been carried out to build a theory of child well-being that is grounded in empirical observations of the empirical sciences—a methodological outlook that chimes with my approach.

But to what extent did the early Confucians employ a concept of well-being at all? We need first to distinguish the concept of happiness from the concept of well-being. For while happiness and well-being are sometimes used interchangeably, the common use of happiness as a psychological condition indicates the need to separate these concepts. In our discussions we will restrict the term 'happiness' to a positive psychological or emotional state rather than the life that is best for someone. Of course, happiness has been used to refer to the highest prudential good by philosophers of the past, and as long as one is clear on what they mean by the term, this is a legitimate way to go on.[7] But in this book, I will follow the current practice and reserve the term 'happiness' to refer to a positive, enduring emotional state.

One might, as Daniel Haybron has done, distinguish well-being from the good life by identifying well-being with one category of value—namely, the prudential or 'good for'—and the good life with a broader class that includes every dimension of value that can be exemplified in one's life.[8] I believe this distinction is much more subtle and difficult than the distinction between happiness and well-being. In fact, it's not a distinction we find among either ancient Greek or Chinese thinkers. For while *eudaimonia* is usually taken as the life that is best for someone (i.e. the highest prudential good), it is also explicitly stated by Aristotle as the most choice-worthy life for humans that combines both virtue or excellence and a host of external goods including friendship and beauty. Within the Confucian tradition, following the *dao* (道 Way) offers us the best human life—the life that all of us ought to aim for—but the Confucians do not make a conceptual distinction between a life that realizes the *dao* and the *prudentially* best life (i.e. the life that is best *for* someone).

It is possible that the Confucians or the Aristotelians were only reflecting on the good life and simply didn't care all that much about the life that is good for a person.[9] A more likely explanation is that they simply thought the best life for you just was the good life (i.e. well-being and the good life are substantially the same). After all, what more can you do you for yourself than obtain a good life? Nevertheless, one might follow Haybron here in wanting to draw a distinction between well-being and the good life because, one might think, one could achieve well-being but not the good life because one is lacking in moral goodness or virtue. This is the main motivation, I take it, for making this distinction. For there are cases, many would claim, where virtue and well-being come apart, which shows that well-being cannot simply be a matter of moral goodness. Edgar Allan Poe captures this point with characteristic elegance:

> In looking at the world *as it is*, we shall find it folly to deny that, to worldly success, a surer path is Villainy than Virtue. What the Scriptures mean by the "*leaven* of unrighteousness" is that leaven by which men *rise*.[10]

On Poe's picture, the vicious, contrary to what ancient thinkers might have thought, can flourish by any reasonable standard. Here the early Confucians, as well as Plato and Aristotle, would contend that while it is true the vicious can gain certain kinds of goods such as wealth, power, fame—what Poe called "worldly success"—they are still missing out on the goods of virtue which are even more central to our well-being. Nothing precludes these thinkers from acknowledging that the vicious can obtain certain desirable goods.

But what really hangs on this dispute? What difference does it make, exactly, if virtue or moral goodness is a fundamental component of well-being, or if it is a fundamental component of the good life but not well-being? A part of the disagreement seems to be rooted in two divergent views about whether moral goodness is non-instrumentally good for you. But determining whether some good is non-instrumentally good for you or merely instrumentally good for you is not always easy. In fact, although this distinction seems to play a key role in every discussion of theorizing about well-being, nobody to my mind has offered a reliable way of distinguishing between these two goods.[11] This is not to deny that these are clearly distinct concepts. But if such a test were available, we could quickly settle certain core disagreements among various well-being theorists. For by using the test to identify any non-pleasure-based goods as carrying non-instrumental value for us, we can clearly rule out (or support) hedonism. A similar strategy would help us determine the truth of desire-based theories or happiness theories.

What is clear is that the early Confucians did not distinguish well-being from the good life. They seemed to be mostly preoccupied by discussions of how one might achieve a virtuous and worthwhile life rather than advancing a theory of well-being, if we are to go along with Haybron's conceptualization. In this way, one might wonder if the whole discussion of the 'Confucian account of well-being' rests on a mistake. After all, the Confucians would insist that what matters is living an excellent life by following the *dao*. As for whether such a life is good or bad *for you*? Who cares?

But such a reply from the Confucians seems unlikely. For if we think about well-being in an intuitive way as the kind of life you want for your children and those you love, or the life that goes well for you, how could the Confucians have simply been unconcerned about it? Confucius himself was certainly striving to bring the *dao* into the world and to turn everyone toward following that path. It strikes me as implausible to think that he would not have thought that such a life would be better for all those following it. A stronger rationale of this claim might be to draw attention to the actual, substantive contents of the Confucian view: do they harmonize with our basic judgments about well-being? Or even if they don't fully do so, can we make sense of their account as offering a prudentially valuable life? While the answer to these questions cannot be answered before exploring the content of their account (a task carried out in subsequent chapters), the Confucian picture of a life lived according to *dao*, constituted by deep and harmonious relationships in healthy families and societies, marked by an enduring state of joy, seems to point toward a picture of human life that is recognizable as good for the people who obtain it.[12]

In this book I take the concept of well-being as the overarching theoretical framework for understanding the ideal life—the life according to the *dao*—represented in the early Confucian texts.[13] Looking at the early Confucian texts through this framework provides an intelligible way to grasp what the Confucians were up to and to understanding the significance of their thoughts.[14] And while I will provide some discussion of contemporary theories of well-being and briefly reflect on how the Confucian view of well-being is related to such theories, my primary aim is not to show that the Confucians held some particular contemporary theory of well-being such as hedonism, the desire account, or perfectionism. For although I do think the Confucians held some form of virtue perfectionism, they don't offer an explicit argument for it, although I think we can build some Confucian-inspired arguments for the position, a task I take up later in Chapter 3.

Rather than offer a *theory* of well-being or the good life, the Confucian tradition offers a reflective account of what makes human lives go well or badly, identifying what they take as good ingredients or elements of human lives, and how they hang together within human communities. Their contribution to the contemporary philosophy of well-being will partly consist in their identification and explanations of certain basic elements or constituents of well-being that Western philosophers have tended to ignore. And if these goods are indeed constitutive of well-being and they cannot be fully explained by certain contemporary theories, then we may also have new arguments against those theories as well.

Contemporary theories of well-being

With some clarification of the concept of well-being and related notions at hand, I want to give a brief overview of the contemporary landscape of well-being. (Those who are familiar with this topic might want to skip ahead.) The aim is to give readers a sense of the field's terrain and to provide enough background for discussing how the Confucian account of well-being can contribute to our contemporary discourse about well-being. But as noted in the Introduction, some recent philosophers have expressed discontent toward the standard theory-building practice, which, as they rightly point out, is not moving toward consensus.[15] I share this sentiment, although I think there is still genuine value in thinking hard about both the positive and negative aspects of each theory, a point they probably wouldn't deny.

In *Reasons and Persons*, Derek Parfit offered the first contemporary welfare taxonomy, which divided theories of well-being into three categories: hedonistic theories, desire-fulfillment theories, and objective list theories.[16] This list has since expanded through the work of other philosophers with the inclusion of the happiness account, hybrid account, and nature-fulfillment account. Each theory, moreover, has become more sophisticated through its attempt to respond to a variety of objections. In the following pages I will briefly describe each of these theories.

Hedonistic theories of well-being take pleasure as the sole constituent of well-being. This view does not imply that nothing except pleasure matters for well-being. The hedonist can very well accept the welfare value of friendship, beauty, or knowledge. But all these things are good for us *because* they give rise to pleasurable experiences; they carry only instrumental prudential value. Take out the pleasure from these things (if that's possible), and they will no longer be good for us.

Desire-fulfillment theories of well-being take the satisfaction of basic (or non-instrumental) desires as the only thing that can be non-instrumentally or non-derivatively good for you. Here desires are construed as a mental state directed at some state of affairs. So if I desire to eat a Godiva truffle, that desire is directed at the state of affairs in which I consume the chocolate. When that state of affairs obtains, my well-being is advanced, at least to some extent. Importantly, the satisfaction condition of desires does not need to include my knowledge of the satisfaction of desire. If I desire that the Cubs win tonight, but I am asleep on the couch when the game ends and the Cubs have won, my desire is still satisfied and my well-being is increased.

The standard objection to desire accounts is that human beings can desire things that seem to be bad for them. One might want to become the president of the United States, for example, only to discover that being president is a terrible experience. We know that satisfying a desire can turn out to actually be harmful to us. Because of this objection, philosophers tend to favor an idealized or informed desire theory, which takes only the satisfaction of idealized or informed desires as what is beneficial to an agent.

While both hedonism and the desire-fulfillment account are often conceived as subjective views because they take well-being as wholly dependent on the mental state of the individual, there is a way in which even hedonism can be construed as an objectivist account because it sees pleasure as the sole prudential good, whatever any individual might think. One could also take this line of thought toward the desire-fulfillment account to conceive it as an objectivist position. But because the content of desires is left wide open, it doesn't seem to make much sense to think of desire accounts as an objectivist view.[17]

Among the objectivist accounts, there are three that hold the most sway for contemporary philosophers: the objective-list account, the nature-fulfillment account, and perfectionism. The objective-list account takes well-being as constituted by a list of objective goods. On the list view, the individual items on the list are not unified by some further goods. (Some have proposed that hedonism is an objective-list account with just one item: pleasure.) The nature-fulfillment account attempts to provide a unified explanation for all the various items that we take as non-instrumentally good for us by appealing to the nature of human beings. On one version, human nature is constituted by various fundamental capacities and characteristic activities. By fulfilling these capacities and engaging in these activities, we flourish as human beings.[18]

Sometimes the term "perfectionism" is used to identify a nature-fulfillment account. But sometimes perfectionism is characterized as a view about well-being that takes virtue or moral goodness as constitutive of well-being. And while one could be a nature-fulfillment theorist and perfectionist (in this sense), the two views can come apart. Perhaps, for example, one believes that the way to fulfill human nature is by exercising dominance and power over others.[19] Or perhaps the perfectionist might claim that virtue has nothing to do with human nature or fundamental capacities.[20]

As those well versed in this philosophical literature knows, there are other theories—such as L. W. Sumner's authentic happiness theory, or the hybrid theory, or Daniel Haybron's self-fulfillment theory—that offer further sophisticated views about well-being. And even the different accounts briefly mentioned earlier come in different versions, sometimes even combining two or more theories.[21] This is not the place to argue for any particular account. As even this brief sketch of the contemporary field reveals, the philosophical literature on this topic is vast and extremely complicated. And as noted earlier, the impasse that seems to mark the current discussion has pushed some philosophers to focus on other topics, such as the mid-level theories proposed by Anna Alexandrova or the vast psychological literature on positive psychology.[22] I will simply give a respectful bow to this literature on philosophical theories of well-being, and mostly work around these debates so that we can focus on the substantive content of the Confucian view. Besides the fact that I don't think there is anything I can say to settle this dispute, the Confucians were simply not in the business of offering a unified theory of well-being, and so to locate their views in one or another theory will not be constructive.

Notes

1 Below I will explore the Chinese character for 'benefit' (*li* 利), because that term seems closely connected to well-being, which is often discussed as what benefits someone. I discuss this issue further in "Well-Being in Early Chinese Philosophy" (forthcoming in *Oxford Handbook of Chinese Philosophy*, ed. Justin Tiwald).

2 See Van Norden (2007: 1–22) for a discussion of these issues. I am largely in agreement with what he says there.

3 See Defoort (2008: 153–181). Carine Defoort, "The Profit That Does Not Profit: Paradoxes with 'Li' in Early Chinese Texts," *Asia Major* 21(1), Third Series (2008), Star Gazing, Firephasing, and Healing in China: Essays in Honor of Nathan Sivin.

4 Unless stated otherwise, all passages from the *Xunzi* are from Eric Hutton, trans., *Xunzi: The Complete Text* (Princeton: Princeton University Press, 2014). For ease of reference, I will simply cite the text as "Xunzi" followed by the chapter number and page number in Hutton's book. The classical Chinese reads: "及至其致好之也，目好之五色，耳好之五聲，口好之五味，心利之有天下。是故權利不能傾也，群眾不能移也，天下不能蕩也。"

5 For a discussion of the distinction between concept and conception, see Rawls (1999: 9).
6 One view endorsed by some philosophers is sometimes called "fragmentation," the view there are multiple concepts of well-being. See Kagan (1994) and Alexandrova (2017).
7 Russell (2012), for example, employs this sense of happiness.
8 For discussions of the distinction between 'well-being' and the 'good life,' see Haybron (2008: 21). Thomas Carson also distinguishes between what is good for me and what is good. See Carson, *Value and the Good Life* (2000: 70–71). Cf. Christopher Heathwood (2010: 653–654).
9 Anne Baril argues against this way of understanding the ancient Greek concept of *eudaimonia* in Baril (2013). See also Daniel Russell's forceful defense of this view in Russell (2012).
10 Poe (1980: 50). Poe seems to capture a more modern sentiment, one that we find denied by many classical thinkers in both China and Greece. Plato argues in his *Republic* that the vicious are ultimately plagued by internal turmoil and cannot flourish.
11 The most prominent way of identifying non-instrumental elements of well-being is by employing various 'tests' or thought-experiments such as the 'crib test' or the 'end-of-life test,' which aim to help identify basic or non-instrumental prudential value. So for example, in the crib test you imagine looking at your child from the perspective of love and think about the kind of life you want for the child. The trouble is that not only will this most likely lump together both non-instrumental or instrumental prudential goods, but the kind of life you envision for the child will also be deeply influenced by a broader set of values you hold which might not help you track the child's well-being.
12 It is worth noting that the *dao* also has a socio-political dimension because the early Confucians believed that the state can and ought to also conform to the Way (邦有道). This relational, communal nature of the *dao* and well-being will be developed in the course of this book as we discuss Confucian virtue, ritual, and family.
13 Olberding (2011) argues that we cannot find an account of flourishing that can play a foundational role in the *Analects*. I think she makes a number of important points, but because I am not arguing for the claim that flourishing or well-being plays a foundational role, I don't think her argument applies here. Moreover, I am also reconstructing an account of well-being that draws on not just the *Analects* (the focus of Olberding's book) but also on the *Mengzi* and *Xunzi*.
14 For a different way of thinking about the role of happiness or well-being in early Chinese philosophy (Xunzi more specifically), see Fraser (2013). Fraser provides an interesting account of happiness in the *Xunzi* that he finds implicit in the text. On Fraser's view, Xunzi (and perhaps other Chinese thinkers) do not provide extended discussions of happiness or well-being because of the focus on the good of the community or society.
15 See Alexandrova (2017) and Bishop (2015).
16 See Parfit (1984: Appendix I).
17 Moreover, all welfare theories purport to be objectively true. Thanks to Hui-chieh Loy for this point.
18 The most sophisticated and well-developed account of this view is provided by Kraut (2007).

19 Thomas Hurka, for example, reads Nietzsche in this way. See Hurka (1993: 3).
20 Christine Swanton defends this kind of position in Swanton (2003).
21 Christopher Heathwood, for example, integrates hedonism with a desire account by taking pleasure as the satisfaction of desire. See Heathwood (2007).
22 Of course, just because there is an impasse with regard to different views does not mean there isn't a correct view.

2   Confucian moral psychology and well-being

A central feature of the Confucian tradition is its practical orientation, and its aim to improve people's lives, both by transforming individuals and building a harmonious society. The early Confucians were especially interested in human motivation, emotion, and behavior—in short, human psychology. After all, given their practical orientation, if their recommendations were ineffective in motivating people to make beneficial changes, then by their lights, their entire project would be a failure.

This chapter provides key elements of early Confucian moral psychology. By identifying their conceptions of human motivation and self-development, I will lay the groundwork for understanding the different goods early Confucians take as central to well-being. Because of their practical orientation, the ethical views of early Confucians tend to emerge from their reflections on human psychology. While this way of approaching ethics opens up Confucian ethics to two distinct kinds of possible criticisms—normative and empirical—it nevertheless chimes well with the growing recognition that our normative theories cannot be detached from facts about human motivations and needs. Owen Flanagan in his pioneering work, *Varieties of Moral Personalities*, dubs this idea the 'Principle of Psychological Realism': "Make sure when constructing a moral theory or projecting a moral ideal that the character, decision processing, and behavior prescribed are possible . . . for creatures like us." (Flanagan 1993: 32)

Any account of morality that focuses on the virtues, then, must also show how the achievement of the virtues is possible for creatures like ourselves. Because moral virtue is a central element of well-being for Confucians, it will be important to dig into the Confucian account of moral psychology and moral development.

While there are different ways of defining the virtues, for our purposes we might characterize it as dispositional qualities of one's character that enable one to feel, think, and act well. On the Confucian account, the virtues would also be structurally connected to various Confucian goods, which will be explained in the course of this book. (Of course, the virtues themselves are a kind of intrinsic good as well.) Because virtues are a kind of psychological state, we need an explanation of how they are developed in the context of a human life and their overall effects on our thoughts and motivations. We need an account of how it is that human beings, psychologically constituted as they are, can do the right thing, move toward virtue, and help build and sustain institutions and communities that are necessary for justice and the common good. Similarly, our account of well-being should be psychologically grounded in the kinds of lives that are achievable by human beings. This doesn't mean that our account of well-being must be something that is *easy* to come by, for it might turn out that well-being requires a host of external conditions (good families, social institutions, political structures) that are hard to develop and sustain. It might also be that the achievement of well-being requires a number of hard-won qualities of character, such as equanimity, optimism, hope, and truthfulness, that may take a long time and great effort to develop. In fact, well-being from the Confucian perspective, because of its emphasis on the acquisition of virtue and well-ordered families and communities, will be difficult to achieve.

The virtues on the early Confucian view are not exactly what contemporary philosophers would want to call 'moral' virtues (i.e. virtues that are aimed at the benefit of others). We do not find in the early Confucians a clear distinction between moral and non-moral virtues—a point that is often made with regard to ancient Greek ethics.[1] This broader way of thinking about the virtues makes it a bit easier to see why moral development would be closely connected to the well-being of individuals. For if moral development is about developing a variety of excellent character traits that help to realize the central goods of well-being, then it will seem more plausible that virtue and well-being are tightly connected.[2]

In assuming a close connection between psychology and normativity, the Confucians make a clear distinction between facts and values. This point is made by A. C. Graham:

> Now the concept of *hsing* 'nature' [*xing* 性] is remarkable in that it seems to be at once factual and normative; we can conceive a living thing's nature both as the course it will follow if uninjured and sufficiently nourished and as the course it ought to follow.
>
> (Graham 2002: 44)

With the exception of Aristotelian nature-fulfillment theorists, most contemporary philosophers who work on well-being reject the view that human nature determines human well-being. But the issue is complex and multi-faceted. Consider the following questions:

1   Is the issue epistemological, metaphysical, or both? Are we talking about whether reflection on human nature is essential for understanding human well-being, or are we claiming that human nature determines (or partially determines) well-being? (The two issues are clearly connected.)

2   Is human nature a normative or non-normative concept? Is it a matter of what, statistically, human beings tend to do in different situations, anchored in our evolutionary history? Or is it a normative notion centered on powers, dispositions, or inclinations of human beings that tend toward the good?

3   Even if there is a connection between human nature and human flourishing, what is the substance of this connection? Does human nature partially *determine* what constitutes a flourishing life, or does it provide only the initial material that constrains the kinds of lives that are possible for humans?

Underlying these questions is the difficult issue concerning the relationship between facts and values, or the descriptive and the normative—a topic that continues to deeply divide philosophers. Interestingly, the early Confucians did not make any sharp distinctions between facts and values and tended to see normativity as built into the natural and social world. This is especially observable in the agricultural metaphors of Mencius (discussed below) as well as the references to the way that the nature of things are closely connected to their good.

Below I will explore a key debate about human nature between Mencius and Xunzi, and how their views mark out two distinctive positions with respect to the relationship between human nature and well-being.[3] Both Mencius and Xunzi offer different ways of conceptualizing human nature that can be fruitfully connected to contemporary developments in moral psychology. By examining this debate, we can sharpen the different conceptual possibilities with regard to the relationship between human nature and well-being.[4]

It should be noted that there is an enormous body of scholarship (in both the East and West) arising from modern and classical commentaries on Mencius and Xunzi's disagreement about human nature, so what I say here will not be able to address all the complexities of the debate. Rather than aiming to settle the debate between Mencius and Xunzi or argue for the correct interpretation of this debate, I will focus on the issues that are philosophically relevant to well-being. We can think about the debate between

Mencius and Xunzi as highlighting important ways nature and culture interact that are significant for well-being. More recent scholarship has also tended toward the direction of noting how both Mencius and Xunzi are drawing our attention to different aspects of our nature that deserve more thought.[5]

But human nature is a challenging topic not only because there seems to be a variety of different concepts associated with 'human nature,' but also because some contemporary philosophers have denied the existence of human nature altogether or argued that even the very use of the concept of human nature ought to be jettisoned because of its racist and sexist history.[6] Dealing with these important difficulties requires its own separate and lengthy treatment. My focus in this chapter is on how the notion of human nature might play a useful role in our understanding of well-being.

One distinction familiar to philosophers is the distinction between 'first nature' and 'second nature.' The distinction goes like this: first nature is constituted by the basic physical and psychological facts that are features of human beings as such. Second nature is those characteristics that human beings develop through habituation and culture. Although I don't think there is a sharp division neatly separating first from second nature, the distinction can help clarify the concept of human nature under discussion, for sometimes any pattern of widespread human activity is taken as exemplifying human nature, for instance waging wars or writing poetry. But such activities are the manifestations of our developed second nature rather than first nature. First nature, rather, equips human beings with certain fundamental drives and tendencies, providing us with the psychological and physiological basis for further development through learning and habituation (thereby forging a second nature). We can think of first nature as providing a broad, formal structure to human life, identifying certain needs of the mind and body, and how human beings in general must undergo the necessary processes of language acquisition, maturation, and healthy socialization.

Any satisfying account of naturalism that builds on an account of human nature must demonstrate how, from the initial conditions set by our basic, first nature, we can come to possess a reflective second nature that enables us to live according to our conception of what is valuable and good. The debate between Mencius and Xunzi deals with both the content of first nature and the relationship between first and second nature. They largely agree about the sort of second nature that we should strive to achieve: a character constituted by the Confucian virtues—in its ultimate form, a sagely life. I now turn to discussing the conception of human nature and moral psychology offered by Mencius and Xunzi. In explicating their views, I will also draw on recent developments in moral psychology.

Mencius on human nature

On Mencius's view, human beings carry certain innate moral tendencies or inclinations, what he calls 'sprouts' (*duan* 端), which are directed toward certain virtues. For Mencius, these inclinations are acquired in the normal course of moral development. He offers the following summary:

> [W]e can see that if one is without the feeling of compassion, one is not human. If one is without the feeling of disdain, one is not human. If one is without the feeling of deference one is not human. If one is without the feeling of approval and disapproval, one is not human. The feeling of compassion is the sprout of benevolence. The feeling of disdain is the sprout of righteousness. The feeling of deference is the sprout of propriety. The feeling of approval and disapproval is the sprout of wisdom. People having these four sprouts is like their having four limbs. To have these four sprouts, yet to claim that one is incapable (of virtue), is to steal from oneself.
>
> (*Mengzi* 2A6)[7]

These four moral sprouts are essential characteristics of human beings. When they are properly cultivated under suitable conditions, they can be developed into the four Confucian virtues of benevolence (*ren* 仁), righteousness (*yi* 義), ritual propriety (*li* 禮), and wisdom (*zhi* 智). One point worth emphasizing is that, while these sprouts carry within them the internal potential to develop into full-blown virtues, the potentiality can be actualized only when a number of conditions are satisfied, including consistent human effort and a proper social environment. To explain this process, Mencius appeals to agricultural metaphors throughout the text, comparing these moral sprouts to barley seeds that ripen only given suitable conditions, such as the right kind of soil, sufficient quantity of rain, and human effort (*Mengzi* 6A7). Similarly, our moral sprouts are also susceptible to a wide range of external conditions that can either nurture or impede their growth. Moral self-cultivation for Mencius primarily consists in strengthening and refining these fundamental moral dispositions through extension, reflection, and study.

So the meaning of Mencius's slogan that "human nature is good" is not that human beings for the most part behave virtuously, but that human beings possess the seeds of goodness that can, given proper conditions, blossom into a virtuous character.

Mencius's use of organic, agricultural metaphors draws attention to certain developmental paths that generate standards of goodness and badness; reflection on such metaphors can also highlight the continuity between humans and the wider natural world. One of the advantages of this form of ethical naturalism, as pointed out by Julia Annas, is that

> the normativity of our ethical discourse is not something which emerges mysteriously with humans and can only be projected back, in an anthropomorphic way, onto trees and their roots. Rather, we find normativity in the realm of living things, plants and animals, already.[8]

In using agricultural metaphors to explain human nature and the moral sprouts, Mencius draws a connection between human beings and the natural world. And while he argues that the nature (*xing*) of humans and other animals are different, he does acknowledge that they have a nature, and therefore, certain norms that apply.[9] Consider the following passage in which Mencius quotes from the Book of Odes (*Shijing*):

> Heaven gives birth to the teeming people.
> If there is a thing, there is a norm.
> This is the constant people cleave to.
> They are fond of this beautiful Virtue.[10]

As Irene Bloom notes in her discussion of Mencius's account of human nature:

> Mencius repeatedly uses agricultural metaphors: images or shoots, seedlings, plants, and trees, and the analogy of organic growth and development—a mode of expression that has the effect of locating human nature in the process of nature as a whole and emphasizing both natural processes and the need for nurture.[11]

The very Chinese character for 'nature' (*xing* 性) is, as A. C. Graham argued, a derivative of the Chinese character *sheng* (生), which means 'to be born, live, or grow.'[12]

Mencius takes our ethical lives as rooted in a number of basic moral emotions constitutive of our nature as humans; unless countervailing forces are present, human beings tend to spontaneously experience them under a range of conditions. Upon seeing a child about to fall into a well, just about all of us will feel the alarm or compassion that Mencius identifies (*Mengzi* 2A6).[13] Feelings of shame might lead one to decline a significant gift (*Mengzi* 6A10). The moral sprouts, even in their uncultivated state, are not merely dormant psychological entities; they play an active role in our psychological economy (Ivanhoe 2002).

Some of these ideas about moral sprouts can be fleshed out by employing contemporary terms and concepts developed in the fields of psychology and cognitive science. For example, the widely discussed 'dual process theory' of cognitive reasoning—an account of cognitive architecture that divides mental operations into two modes or 'systems'—suggests that the Mencian sprouts are more closely connected to the fast, intuitive, and 'hot' automatic system ('System 1') rather than the slow, deliberative, and 'cool' reasoning system ('System 2') which together regulate both the cognitive and affective qualities of our mental lives (Kahneman 2011).[14] As noted in the preceding examples, in certain morally charged situations the Mencian sprouts trigger certain emotions such as compassion, shame, or disapproval. Mencius offers a vivid illustration of this phenomenon:

> Now, in the past ages, there were those who did not bury their parents. When their parents died, they took them and abandoned them in a gulley. The next day they passed them, and foxes were eating them, bugs were sucking on them. Sweat broke out on the survivors' foreheads. They turned away and did not look. It was not for the sake of others that they sweated. What was inside their hearts broke through to their countenances. So they went home and, returning with baskets and shovels, covered them.
>
> (*Mengzi* 3A5)

The emotionally charged reactions upon seeing the corpses of the parents are swift and spontaneous—not the result of rational deliberation (System 2).

This is not to say that the two systems work in isolation; although each has its own distinctive function, they interact in important ways. For example, System 1 can relay feelings and intuitions to System 2, and System 2 can take those feelings and intuitions, process them, and endorse or reject them, resulting (sometimes) in action. Because on the Confucian ethical worldview much of the moral substance of our lives depends on how well (or badly) we react in everyday social encounters, Mencius was sensitive to the process of nurturing these sprouts and fine-tuning our emotional tendencies. Below we will explore what role System 2 (in the form of *zhi* or practical wisdom) plays in the development of the sprouts.

Philosophers have recently started to explore the extent to which Mencius's moral psychology can be characterized in terms of moral modularity.[15] Moral modules, to give a brief description, are cognitive-affective-conative dispositions that are activated automatically, cognitively impenetrable (i.e. difficult to manipulate through rational control), and triggered by a narrow range of inputs (domain specific).[16] For example, we might posit a 'care module' that operates under certain conditions (e.g. seeing a toddler run into a busy street). As Mencius notes, we feel an immediate sense of concern in such situations that arise in us spontaneously. The care module helps to explain why we have such experiences.

While there are good reasons for not attributing a strong conception of moral modularity to Mencius—what Flanagan calls a "modules-all-the-way-up and all-the-way-down" view because of the way that practical wisdom (*zhi*) can influence the shape and development of the sprouts, Mencius's conception of the sprouts as offering independent affective bases for specific virtues suggests that he believed in certain domain-specific moral competencies that are innate to humans and foundational for morality.[17] For this reason, even if Mencius cannot be interpreted as endorsing a view of moral modularity without qualification, contemporary discussion of moral modularity can serve as a useful tool for understanding Mencius's views, and Mencius, in turn, may offer fruitful ways of exploring modular-based ethical views.

Identifying Mencius as offering the first expression of a modular-based moral view, Flanagan (2014) draws intriguing comparisons between what he calls Mencian Moral Modularity (MMM) and a contemporary version of moral modularity proposed by Jonathan Haidt and his colleagues, known as Moral Foundations Theory (MFT).[18] Both pictures present an account of morality that arises out of a set of innate emotional dispositions that furnish us with the basic moral architecture that constitutes our 'first nature.' Earlier we identified the four moral inclinations (compassion, shame, deference, approval/disapproval) that Mencius takes as basic. On Hadit's MFT there are five distinct moral domains: (1) harm/care; (2) fairness/reciprocity; (3) ingroup/loyalty; (4) authority/respect; and (5) purity/sanctity. (Haidt now endorses a sixth foundation, 'liberty/oppression,' but believes there is less evidence for it than the aforementioned five foundations.)[19] On Haidt's view, these domains offer us five moral (or proto-moral) inclinations or tendencies that have become embedded in our nature through evolution, allowing us to develop distinct moral competencies and skills. What Mencius's sprout view and Haidt's MFT view hold in common is the idea that human beings have certain moral inclinations as part of their basic equipment, and that morality largely consists in developing, modifying, and reconfiguring these basic moral dispositions. While culture, as both views would emphasize, plays a crucial role in shaping these sprouts or modules, our moral lives must ultimately be built on top of this foundation.

The basic moral modules are, Haidt contends, like the five taste receptors that allowing us to distinguish and make judgments about different tastes. Just as the taste receptors allow us to mark out different tastes—'Sour!' 'Sweet!'—moral receptors allow us to identify and react to a wide range of moral phenomena: 'Shame on him!' 'How heroic!' This analogy between morality and taste, as Haidt acknowledges, was also suggested by Mencius (as well as by Hume):

> Hence, I say that mouths have the same preferences in flavors, ears have the same preferences in sounds, eyes have the same preferences in attractiveness. When it comes to hearts, are they alone without preferences in common? What is it that hearts prefer in common? I say that it is order and righteousness. The sages first discovered what our hearts prefer in common. Hence, order and righteousness delight our hearts like meat delights our mouths.
>
> (*Mengzi* 6A7)

Extending this point, we can conceive of Mencius's moral sprouts as distinct moral receptors that allow us to grasp and evaluate different moral situations. Each moral sprout allows us to feel and judge in ways that are appropriate to different domains of moral experience; the sprouts charge our experiences with a normative pull. Confronted with rude behavior, we react with contempt; upon seeing a child fall, we're moved with pity. Of course, our moral experience can be much more complex than these descriptions suggest because we can experience a number of different feelings at once: I feel both angry and sad that you would do that to me; I'm both grateful for and ashamed by that kind gesture. Different sprouts can activate at the same time and pull us in different directions.

But how do we know if the moral sprouts are growing properly? What's the ideal configuration for the sprouts? It is important to remember that the sprouts are not virtues. As the agricultural metaphor of 'sprouts' suggests, the Mencian sprouts are in need of care and attention. What we are after, so to speak, is a moral harvest: a mature and cultivated self. The metaphor of farming, rather than vegetation, seems more apt. Farming itself is an outstanding product of human culture requiring patience, wisdom, and effort (Ivanhoe 2013). This suggests the need for a more centralized reasoning process—System 2—that can offer normative guidance through rational deliberation. Indeed, as scholars have pointed out, Mencius's fourth sprout of 'approval and disapproval'—which is directed toward the virtue of 'wisdom' (*zhi*)—seems to carry a more cognitive orientation (Kim 2010). One can construe Mencian wisdom as a 'meta-virtue' that allows us to reflectively guide the development of the other sprouts: "The core of benevolence is serving one's parents. The core of righteousness is obeying one's elder brother. The core of wisdom is knowing these two and not abandoning them."[20] By opening space for normative reflection, Mencius's moral theory can more effectively represent our intuitively held normative judgments than the kind of modular-based view advocated by Haidt that takes rationality as merely allowing for post hoc rationalizations. In this way, Mencius offers a way to integrate certain attractive features of Haidt's moral psychology (while avoiding its excesses) with the conceptual resources for preserving normative theorizing within a naturalized framework. Returning to the distinction between first and second nature, Mencius's sprouts give some content to first nature and show how it has a tendency toward a developed, virtuous second nature.

Allowing room for reflection and practical wisdom makes Mencius's moral theory more plausible. But it also shows that Mencius's sprouts cannot be conceived in a strongly modular way because it seems that the development of the sprout of approval and disapproval both influences, and is also influenced by, the other sprouts—calling into question their cognitive impenetrability. (Briefly, cognitive impenetrability requires that the modules are fairly well insulated from the influences of reasoning and deliberation.) On the other hand, some cognitive scientists like Dan Sperber have defended less strict ways of understanding modularity.

Mencius offers a conception of first nature constituted not only by basic bodily desires for comfort, food, and sex but also by a variety of moral inclinations that through education and culture can develop into a fully developed moral second nature. One might wonder, however, about the way that first nature also seems to be constituted by nastier impulses—the "weeds," we might call them, following Owen Flanagan.[21] Consider Aleksandr Solzhenitsyn's darker (though still hopeful) account of human nature:

> Gradually it was disclosed to me that the line separating good and evil passes not through states, nor between classes, nor between political parties either—but right through every human heart—and through all human hearts. This line shifts. Inside us, it oscillates with the years. And even within hearts overwhelmed by evil, one small bridgehead of good is retained. And even in the best of all hearts, there remains . . . an unprooted small corner of evil.
>
> (Solzhenitsyn 1974: 615)

We will explore this darker picture of human beings as a mixed bag of good and evil when we turn to Xunzi (although 'evil' isn't quite what he ascribes to human nature). Solzhenitsyn follows a long line of thinkers, including Thomas Hobbes and Fyodor Dostoyevsky, who have keenly observed the various twisted aspects of human beings. One might worry that Mencius's account of human nature was distorted by a Pollyannaish view of the world. But Mencius did not live in a fantasyland populated by sages and saints. He lived in early China during the Warring States period—a time of political strife, social upheaval, and violent wars. Mencius was not claiming that human beings *are* generally benevolent and good, but that they are equipped with the moral resources to develop virtues: they can *become* benevolent and good. What explains the badness of human beings is at least partially due to the social environment as well as the way that our non-moral desires can powerfully drive us toward vice. Mencius believed that our natural appetitive desires for things like food, sex, bodily comfort, and other kinds of basic pleasures are also fundamental components of human nature.

This more expansive conception of human nature allows Mencius to identify not only the four moral sprouts as basic features of human beings that can sometimes give rise to bad behavior, but also pick out basic bodily and psychological desires as possible sources of distorted character traits. But, Mencius would claim, none of these moral or non-moral desires are in themselves bad; they all have a proper place within the space of human life. Each non-moral desire, for example, is directed at some recognizable good or goods within the human life-form: the desire for food aims at health, the desire for sex aims at romantic union and children, and the desire for bodily comfort aims at physical security.

Employing this train of ideas, Mencius might have argued in the following way: each vicious trait such as racial hatred can be broken down into either one of the four sprouts or a basic non-moral desire, and in their basic, root form, such inclinations point toward a genuine good, despite their sensitivity to external conditions that can easily lead them to become misdirected. Problems arise when the basic desires or inclinations are disordered—for example, by attributing to them more weight than is appropriate. What is necessary, Mencius thought, is to properly organize the various desires or inclinations, with greater focus being placed on the "greater part" of our nature (i.e. the inclinations toward virtue):

> People care for each part of themselves. They care for each part, so they nurture each part. There is not an inch of flesh they do not care for, so there is not an inch of flesh that they do not nurture. But if we want to examine whether someone is good or not, there is no other way than considering what they choose to nurture. The body has esteemed and lowly parts; it has great and petty parts. One does not harm the great parts for the sake of the petty parts. One does not harm the esteemed parts for the sake of the lowly parts. One who nurtures the petty parts becomes a petty person. One who nurtures the great parts becomes a great person. Suppose there is a gardener who abandons his mahogany tree but nurtures his date tree. Then he is a lowly gardener.

One who unthinkingly ignores his back while taking care of his finger is a rabid wolf. . . . It is not the function of the ears and eyes to reflect, and they are misled by things. Things interact with other things and simply lead them along. But the function of the heart is to reflect. If it reflects, then it will get it. If it does not reflect, then it will not get it. This is what Heaven has given us. If one first takes one's stand on what is greater, then what is lesser will not be able to snatch it away.

(Mengzi 6A14–15)

In the latter part of this passage, Mencius makes two significant remarks. The first is that our non-moral desires, due to their non-rational character, can easily mislead us. The second is that 'reflection' (*si* 思) is necessary to grasp the proper weight that should be attached to the various aspects of our nature, with the greatest weight being attributed to our moral inclinations.[22] The first comment returns us to the question of why Mencius believed that the vicious traits we find in people are not constitutive of human nature. The reason, as Mencius suggests, is that our appetitive desires of the 'lower part,' while serving an important function in life, can easily lead us to act badly and live a 'petty' human life. (Mencius elsewhere describes such a life as 'tragic'; *Mengzi* 6A11.3.) So although we can observe frequent cases of bad behavior, Mencius offers an 'account of error'—an explanation of why, given that our basic inclinations are directed toward the good, it is so easy to fall into moral depravity. This account reveals why the moral vices are not fundamental features of human nature but an improper outgrowth of basic inclinations that are in themselves good. Mencius develops this story further by pointing out the various ways in which our cultural and social environment can impede us from proper moral growth. In a number of passages, Mencius draws attention to how an improper environment can affect our character:

> Mengzi said, "The trees of Ox Mountain were once beautiful. But because it bordered on a large state, hatchets and axes besieged it. Could it remain verdant? Due to the respite it got during the day and night, and the moisture of rain and dew, there were sprouts and shoots growing there. But oxen and sheep came and grazed on them. Hence, it was as if it were barren. Seeing it barren, people believed that there had never been any timber there. But could this be the nature of the mountain?
>
> When we consider what is present in people, could they truly lack the hearts of benevolence and righteousness? The way that they discard their genuine hearts is like the hatchets and axes in relation to the trees.

With them besieging it day by day, can it remain beautiful? . . . Others see that he is an animal, and think that there was never any capacity there. But is this what a human is like inherently?"

(Mengzi 6A8.1–8.2)

The metaphor of Ox Mountain illustrates how external forces can devastate the developmental process of moral growth in a way that makes human beings appear to not only lack the capacity for morality but even to naturally harbor vice. By drawing attention to this possibility, Mencius defends his view that our hearts carry a moral orientation and a natural tendency toward goodness.

Mengzi said, "In years of plenty, most young men are gentle; in years of poverty, most young men are violent. It is not that the potential that Heaven confers on them varies like this. They are like this because of what sinks and drowns their hearts. Consider barley. Sow the seeds and cover them. The soil is the same and the time of planting is also the same. They grow rapidly, and by the time of the summer solstice they have all ripened. Although there are some differences, these are due to the richness of the soil and to unevenness in the rain and in human effort."

(Mengzi 6A7)

Although barley seeds carry the potential for developing into a ripe harvest, the soil quality, climate patterns, and human effort are all significant factors that constitute the necessary conditions for proper growth. Mencius takes the development of human character, even with its direction toward goodness, as requiring the satisfaction of a host of conditions for full maturation. And although he does not offer a detailed analysis of exactly which social conditions must be met for the proper development of the moral sprouts, he identifies certain plausible conditions, for example freedom from poverty along with opportunities for education and work.[23] Given his Confucian commitments, he would have endorsed a good familial environment as well.

Taking up the basic account of human nature and psychology Mencius offers, we may state Mencius's account of well-being as one that takes the development of human nature, especially the moral sprouts, as central to the achievement of a flourishing human life. In developing these sprouts into virtues, we hone our emotional dispositions in ways that enable us to live well in family and society. So developing these sprouts also requires that a number of prerequisite conditions be satisfied: to become fully virtuous people, we need good families and communities and a culture that prizes certain values such as filial piety. There are, Mencius also acknowledges, other natural desires for comfort, good food, and sex that should also be satisfied in proper ways, in ways that help support the growth of the sprouts. And just as these sprouts develop through a certain internally structured process directed toward certain ends, human lives are also directed toward certain ends, such as a sound moral character and well-ordered life in the family. On Mencius's account, it is by achieving these ends that we realize Confucian well-being.

Xunzi on human nature

Xunzi denies certain key elements of Mencius's moral psychology, especially the existence of moral inclinations that can be guided to move human beings toward virtue. Whereas Mencius believed that to achieve virtue we need to build up the various moral tendencies that are latent in our hearts, Xunzi believes that human nature primarily consists of powerful, egoistic tendencies aimed at private acquisition, rather than other-regarding actions. Thus, Xunzi's claim that "people's nature is bad" (人之性惡):

> Now people's nature is such that they are born with a fondness for profit in them. If they follow along with this, then struggle and contention will arise, and yielding and deference will perish therein. They are born with feelings of hate and dislike in them. If they follow along with these, then cruelty and villainy will arise, and loyalty and trustworthiness will perish therein. They are born with desires of the eyes and ears, a fondness for beautiful sights and sounds. If they follow along with these, then lasciviousness and chaos will arise, and ritual and *yi* [righteousness 義], proper form and order, will perish therein. Thus, if people follow along with their inborn dispositions and obey their nature, they are sure to come to struggle and contention, turn to disrupting social divisions and order, and end up becoming violent.
>
> (*Xunzi*, Ch. 28: 248)

As many scholars have pointed out, Xunzi's main point here is not to highlight how terrible human beings are but to emphasize how many of our natural tendencies and inclinations, if left unregulated and not properly channeled through intelligent guidance, will lead toward disorder and harm. Accordingly, Xunzi makes great efforts to emphasize the role of human intention, deliberation, and artifice.

There is disagreement among scholars concerning Xunzi's understanding of human nature and whether Xunzi's concept of nature (*xing* 性) is the same as Mencius's concept of nature. A number of scholars have argued that because Xunzi's concept of human nature is quite different from the concept Mencius holds, that the disagreement between them is really just terminological.[24] Some have also held that the Chinese term *xing* does not correspond to our concept of 'nature.'[25] Here I will bypass this debate and rely on a definition of *xing* attributed to Xunzi by Siufu Tang that I think broadly captures what Xunzi had in mind: "*Xing* [nature] is the underlying cause of natural development and natural occurrences of life. Yet natural life occurrences, including natural faculties, responses, likes and dislikes, are also called *xing*."[26] An appeal to human nature can help explain various natural developments (e.g. learning of language or physical growth). But we use the term 'human nature' to refer to both what explains these events and also to refer to these events as an aspect of human nature, similar to the way we might say that language-acquisition is a part of human nature and that learning a language is natural to humans. This characterization seems to overlap considerably with Mencius's concept of nature (*xing*) and corresponds well enough to our concept of 'human nature' for our purposes.

To become virtuous, on Xunzi's view, we need to reshape and build into our character those moral values and dispositions that will enable us to live according to the *dao*. Despite Xunzi's view that human beings are naturally inclined toward self-absorption and vice, he is confident that we all possess the capacity to become a sage, which can be realized by undergoing a long, arduous process of moral development consisting in ritual practices, obedience to a teacher, and recitation of the classics. Like a piece of metal capable of being forged into a sharp blade through a long process of repeated blows, Xunzi sees our nature as capable of taking on a determinate moral shape through a long and steady course of moral development:

> Not giving up is where success resides. If you start carving and give up, you will not be able to break even rotten wood, but if you start carving and do not give up, then you can engrave even metal and stone.
> (*Xunzi*, Ch. 1: 4)

What Xunzi denies, contra Mencius, is the existence of innate dispositions that are directed toward virtue. Whereas Mencius favors the use of organic, agricultural metaphors (which draw attention to the natural, innate tendencies that can be cultivated into morally good characteristics), Xunzi favors craft metaphors, drawing attention to the way that recalcitrant materials such as wood or metal, devoid of any internal principle of growth, can be shaped and reformed to fit our desired ends through rational guidance:

> Through steaming and bending, you can make wood as straight as an ink-line into a wheel. And after its curve conforms to the compass, even

when parched under the sun it will not become straight again, because the steaming and bending have made it a certain way. Likewise, when wood comes under the ink-line, it becomes straight, and when metal is brought to the whetstone, it becomes sharp. The gentleman learns broadly and examines himself thrice daily, and then his knowledge is clear and his conduct is without fault.

(*Xunzi*, Ch. 1: 1)

Unlike sprouts that carry an internal principle of growth and maturation, a piece of wood or metal does not have a natural tendency toward taking on a particular shape. In appealing to such metaphors, Xunzi is denying Mencius's view that there is a natural tendency for human beings to move toward virtue. But although Xunzi does not believe that we can rely on human nature to develop into moral beings, our nature is such that, given time and pressure, we can become reliably good. One of the keys to this developmental process for Xunzi is ritual or rite (*li* 禮), which Benjamin Schwartz describes as referring to "all those 'objective' prescriptions of behavior, whether involving rite, ceremony, manners, or general deportment, that bind human beings and spirits together in networks of interacting roles within the family, within human society, and with the numinous realm beyond."[27] (We will return to the significance of ritual in virtue acquisition in Chapter 3.) For Xunzi, it is human artifice, culture, and education that are wholly responsible for developing the virtues and obtaining a good life.

While Xunzi insists that the virtues that we can develop are not, even in some primordial form, constitutive of our nature as humans, he is not denying that human nature matters for moral development:

Someone asks: ritual and *yi* [righteousness] and the accumulation of deliberate effort are people's nature, and that is why the sage is able to produce them. I answer: this is not so. The potter mixes clay and produces tiles. Yet, how could the clay of the tiles be the potter's nature? The craftsman carves wood and makes utensils. Yet, how could the wood of the utensils be the craftsman's nature? The relationship of the sage to ritual and *yi* can be compared to mixing up clay and producing things.

(*Xunzi*, Ch. 23: 253)

Xunzi anticipates an objection here that is sometimes made against those who deny that human nature is normatively significant: that without an account of human nature, one's account of morality or well-being will not be realizable for human beings. But Xunzi would readily agree that first human nature, as the basic psychological and physiological stuff that can be transformed through ritual and training, is relevant to our understanding of the developmental process of human beings and the kind of life that human beings are capable of. After all, if the constitution of human beings were incapable of taking on the Confucian virtues, it would be pointless to promote their achievement.

Xunzi acknowledges that the necessary stuff for becoming virtuous is already present in human nature: "thus, it is clear that the material for understanding these things and the equipment for practicing them is present in people on the street" (*Xunzi*, Ch. 23: 254). But aren't we now just back to Mencius's view that human beings have the sprouts of virtue already within their nature? What is the disagreement here between Mencius and Xunzi? In fact, a number of prominent scholars have questioned the extent to which their views about human nature conflict.[28]

There is indeed substantial overlap between the views of Mencius and Xunzi, but there remain two important points on which they disagree that carry significant implications:

1   There exist moral sprouts inherent in human nature that tend toward virtue.
2   The content of human nature is normatively significant; there is an end or a set of ends determined by our nature that human beings should pursue.

Points (1) and (2) bear a close connection because the truth of (1) seems to support the truth of (2) by showing how human nature is directed toward a virtuous life. Xunzi seems to deny (2) by arguing against (1). So on Xunzi's view, even with the moral sprouts that Mencius posits, human beings would still need much external guidance. But this point does not require the denial of (2) because it is about the necessary social conditions for achieving virtue and is not a denial of the claim that human nature fixes certain ends. This also isn't a point that Mencius would deny, for while Mencius doesn't emphasize rituals or teachers as Xunzi did, he clearly does acknowledge the importance of external conditions that need to be satisfied. So I think we can still hold that the disagreement about (2) really comes down to their disagreement about (1).[29] In the next section, I will explore how these points of contention are philosophically relevant to the discussion of well-being and are connected to contemporary findings in developmental psychology.

Contemporary significance of the debate between Mencius and Xunzi

By reflecting on Mencius and Xunzi's debate about human nature, we can extrapolate two divergent ways of thinking about the role of human nature in normative inquiry and locate the central empirical thesis on which their views hinge. I call the first way of thinking about human nature's role, advocated by Mencius, as *strong determination*:

> *Strong determination*: The content of human nature determines an end or set of ends that must be achieved to obtain a flourishing life.

By contrast, Xunzi advocates what I will call *weak determination*:

> *Weak determination*: The content of human nature restricts the kinds of lives that are possible for human beings but does not fix any end or set of ends that must be satisfied to achieve a flourishing life.

Weak determination, however, does not imply that there are no objectively good ends that human beings must pursue to achieve a flourishing life. What it does mean is that *human nature* is not what determines the content of human flourishing, although human nature might generate some content restrictions.[30]

Earlier I argued that Mencius and Xunzi would have taken the truth of strong or weak determination as dependent on the existence of the sorts of moral sprouts Mencius posited. But that cannot be the whole story because even if the moral sprouts existed, there remains a further question about whether there are other inclinations inherent in human nature that are directed toward vices, which I earlier called weeds. If these weeds are much stronger and more widespread than the sprouts, it becomes difficult to see why human nature determines any particular good end(s), unless we simply beg the question in favor of the moral sprouts as constituting what is normatively significant about human nature.

On the other hand, one could simply reject the strong/weak determination framework altogether and argue that, even if the only inclinations human beings had were geared toward virtues, human nature is still not what justifies the pursuit of the virtues; rather, the virtues are good to pursue because of their goodness. Such a view might be held by a welfare objective list theorist.

But a central challenge to the objective list theory is that they merely provide a list of goods without any underlying principle, which makes questions about what items to include or exclude from that list seemingly arbitrary. Independent of the force of this objection, I think it can be agreed that if there was a principle or unifying thread to the various items within the objective list, we would have a more satisfying account of virtue. The problem, as objective list theorists see it, is that human nature simply can't fulfill that task. But reflecting on the preceding discussion, it seems that if human nature consisted of good inclinations and dispositions, then human nature would be more tightly connected to human goods. A crucial issue turns on the truth of the antecedent of this conditional statement.

There has been a substantial amount of empirical support for the view that certain moral inclinations are constitutive of human nature. One of the pioneers of research on early moral development, Michael Tomasello, comments:

> [F]rom around their first birthday—when they first begin to walk and talk and become truly cultural beings—human children are already cooperative and helpful in many, though obviously not all, situations. And they do not learn this from adults; it comes naturally.
>
> (Tomasello 2009: 4)

Paul Bloom and his colleagues at the Yale Infant Cognition Center have also conducted ingenious experiments on babies as young as five months old, and they argue that

> the right theory of our moral lives has two parts. It starts with what we are born with, and this is surprisingly rich: babies are moral animals, equipped by evolution with empathy and compassion, the capacity to judge the actions of others, and even some rudimentary understanding of justice and fairness. But we are more than just babies. A critical part of our morality—so much of what makes us human—emerges over the course of human history and individual development. It is the product of our compassion, our imagination, and our magnificent capacity for reason.
>
> (Bloom 2013: 218)

These comments provide some empirical support for Mencius's views about the moral sprouts, but it is worth noting how Bloom's final comments also acknowledge a point that Xunzi goes to great length to defend, which is that the accumulation of cultural capital, and our own individual abilities to reason and deliberate, are critical for becoming full-fledged moral agents.

An overall picture of the moral life of babies emerges from the last several decades of research in developmental psychology: it is much more rich and complex than we had realized, and they are naturally equipped with certain basic moral emotions. The research suggests that something like what Mencius understood as moral sprouts really do seem constitutive of human nature. It bears emphasizing, however, that these moral sensibilities that we find in babies are fledgling and underdeveloped; perhaps they might be better thought of as *proto-moral* rather than moral, and one might argue that because the process of development requires so much external input they should not be taken as directed toward a virtuous life. Xunzi would likely have offered such a response, and it has been forcefully articulated by Eric Hutton.[31] Indeed, there remains considerable work that needs to be done to take those primitive, fledgling inclinations of babies and develop them into reliable and well-ordered moral inclinations. Left on their own without external regulation and guidance, it would be practically impossible for the children to become virtuous agents. We can draw an analogy here with our linguistic capacity, which is widely accepted as innate. It too is quite underdeveloped in babies and requires extensive social and cultural input if it is to develop into a refined ability to speak and understand a particular language. But the acknowledgement of such extensive external input does not seem to undermine the fact that our linguistic capacity is inherent in human nature, which we must develop naturally for the process of language acquisition to begin at all.

When it comes to the existence of certain natural moral inclinations or dispositions—Mencius's moral sprouts—it seems that Mencius enjoys greater empirical support than Xunzi. But what Xunzi grasped more clearly—perhaps a point of greater practical importance—is just how hard virtue is to obtain. Because in Xunzi's view we lacked the internal resources to cultivate virtue, we must rely heavily on external support and daily, constant self-monitoring, along with a community of moral support, to make sure we do not deviate from the correct path.

Mencius and Xunzi's agreements are deeper and more substantial than their disagreements. They both agree that certain Confucian virtues such as ritual propriety, benevolence, and filial piety are necessary for both individual and communal well-being. Both thinkers, therefore, accept some form of virtue perfectionism: the view that virtue is a fundamental component or constituent of well-being. But does one of their views of human nature and moral psychology fit better with virtue perfectionism than another?

In my view, Mencius's understanding of human nature as constituted by basic moral inclinations provides more support for virtue perfectionism than does Xunzi's view. This is because if there really are moral sprouts that are directed toward particular virtues, we must develop these virtues in order to find psychological fulfillment. And because psychological happiness is a constituent of human flourishing, it looks like the development of the virtues will also be positively connected to well-being. It seems that on Mencius's view, virtues are foundational to what it is to be human, and so the development and exercise of the virtues are closely connected to self-actualization, which in turn is closely tied to well-being.

The worry about Xunzi's position is that by seeing human nature as not having morally directed inclinations, it is not clear how he could maintain that the virtues are a fundamental component of well-being, for it seems that for Xunzi human nature can be reformed to connect with a vast and diverse range of ends that may even be antithetical to morality. Now in fact, Xunzi does think that developing the virtues will, in the long-run, lead to the most satisfying life. But what is not clear is why exactly this is so, because human beings are not actually geared toward a moral life. And while it might be the case that developing moral desires and virtues provide the instrumental means for best satisfying one's non-moral desires, this would not get us to the claim that virtues are constitutive of well-being in the way that Xunzi clearly seems to think they are.[32] But perhaps there is a further story that Xunzi could tell here about how in the beginning one starts by only seeking to be virtuous because of non-moral considerations, eventually (through the practice of ritual) one comes to appreciate the moral goodness for its own sake and becomes constitutive of one's own good. It does seem, however, that Mencius's picture provides a smoother psychological account that shows how even our basic first nature was tending toward a virtuous life all along.

Notes

1 This fact seems to support the views of philosophers such as Elizabeth Anscombe (Anscombe 1958) and Bernard Williams (1985), that 'morality' is a modern invention. We observe one reason why the study of non-Western ethics is important: they help draw attention to those aspects of our own moral thought and practice that may very well be idiosyncratic.

2 Here we see that the concept of virtue for the early Confucians bears a closer connection to more Aristotelian or eudaemonist accounts of virtue than Humean or some modern accounts, by connecting virtue to flourishing. But for a sentimentalist account of Mencius, see Liu (2003).

3 It is worth noting that I use the term "human nature" to translate *xing* (性), which some scholars have found problematic. See Ames (1991) and Robins (2011). Admittedly, there are always bound to be some difficulties with any translation of a term, but the real issue is whether there is sufficient overlap between the two terms for productive discourse. I believe the descriptions given of *xing* by Mencius and Xunzi offer enough evidence of significant overlap. Moreover, given that the practice of translating *xing* as 'human nature' is widespread among many eminent scholars of the Chinese philosophy, I believe my use is well justified. See Graham (2002), Schwartz (1985), Bloom (1997), Shun (1997), Ivanhoe (1990), and Van Norden (2007).

4 Confucius was notoriously vague about human nature and leaves its content open-ended, and so the connection between well-being and human nature as envisioned by Confucius is not entirely clear. Amy Olberding discusses the idea of human nature in the Analects in her insightful book, *Moral Exemplars in the Analects*. See Olberding (2011: 45–49).

5 See Wong (2015).

6 Louise M. Antony discusses some of the bad history of sexist appeals to human nature in Antony (2013).

7 All translation of the *Mengzi* (Mencius) are from Van Norden (2008).
8 Annas (2005).
9 See *Mengzi* 6A3.
10 *Mengzi* 6A6. It is notable that there is also an appeal to the workings of Heaven (*tian*). Focusing on this point can lead to an interpretation of Mencius as endorsing a form of natural law theory.
11 Bloom (1997: 24).
12 Graham (2002).
13 There is a question here about the extent to which compassion is the emotion that Mencius identifies, particularly in the famous "child and the well" thought experiment. It might be that the heart of 'compassion' (*ce yin zhi xin* 惻 隱 之 心) gives rise to a more rudimentary emotion like alarm or distress. See Kim-chong (2007: 45) and also Kim (2010).
14 While I find the dual-process theory in some ways illuminating and employ it here, I suspect that the story of how our mind works is much more complicated. What the theory does nicely is distinguish between two forms of mental processes.
15 Flanagan and Williams (2010), Flanagan (2014), Flanagan (2017: Ch. 3), Seok (2008).
16 Exactly what moral modules are is a complex issue. Jonathan Haidt (Haidt 2012: 401–402) rejects the stricter criteria for modularity proposed by Jerry Fodor (1983) and endorses a looser conception endorsed by Sperber and Hirschfeld (2004) and Sperber (2005). For a treatment of modularity in general, see Fodor (1983) and Sperber (1994).
17 Seok (2008).
18 For discussions of the modular nature of Haidt's theory, see Haidt and Bjorklund (2008: 204–206) and Haidt (2012: 144–148).
19 See Haidt (2012: 197–205) for discussion of the liberty/oppression foundation.
20 *Mengzi* 4A27. Bryan Van Norden also characterizes wisdom as a meta-virtue. See Van Norden (2008:101).
21 See Flanagan (2017: Ch. 5).
22 Another important concept in Mencius's moral system connected to reflection is *zhi* (智) or 'wisdom,' one of the four Mencian virtues. As noted earlier, one function of *zhi* is to allow reflection on the other virtues as a sort of 'meta-virtue.' See Owen Flanagan's discussion in Flanagan (2017: 90–95).
23 See *Mengzi* 1A7. It might be noted that there are extraordinary cases (Sage-King Shun) who grew up under terrible conditions but nevertheless succeeded. We might say then that these conditions apply characteristically rather than necessarily. I thank Youngsun Back for this point.
24 See, for example, Graham (2002) and Goldin (1999: 290).
25 See Ames (1991) and Robins (2011).
26 Tang (2016: 171).
27 Schwartz (1985: 67). See also Fingarette (1972).
28 See Lau (2000), Cua (1977), and Graham (1989). While these scholars do not reject any sort of disagreement about human nature between Mencius and Xunzi, they do raise reasons for thinking that the disagreement isn't as significant as it might initially appear.
29 It is worth noting a relevant passage that might seem to suggest that even if Xunzi accepted (1), he would still reject (2): "As for people, even if they had a fine nature and inborn substance and their hearts were keenly discriminating

and wise, they would still need to seek worthy teachers to serve, and choose worthy friends to befriend" (*Xunzi*, Ch. 23: 257). But on closer examination, this passage allows for both the acceptance of (1) and the acceptance of (2) because teachers or friends might be instrumentally necessary for achieving the end(s) set by nature. In fact, I believe there is good reason to think even Mencius would have accepted this remark.

30 This leaves open the possibility that Xunzi was an objectivist about well-being, which is how I interpret him. But rather than human nature determining human flourishing, Xunzi seems to think that it is the Way (*dao*) that determines what constitutes human flourishing. There is, however, controversy about whether Xunzi was a constructivist or a realist. For a defense of the realist position, see Eric Hutton, "Ethics in the *Xunzi*," in Eric Hutton (ed.) *Dao Companion to the Philosophy of Xunzi*; Kurtis Hagen defends a constructivist view in *The Philosophy of Xunzi: A Reconstruction* (Chicago: Open Court, 2007). For an agnostic view, see David Wong, "Xunzi's Metaethics," in Eric Hutton (ed.) *Dao Companion to the Philosophy of Xunzi* (Dordrecht: Springer, 2016). I thank Eirik Harris for pushing me to reflect more on this issue.

31 Eric Hutton, "Does Xunzi Have a Consistent Theory of Human Nature?" in T. C. Kline III and Philip J. Ivanhoe (eds.) *Virtue, Nature, and Moral Agency in the Xunzi* (Indianapolis: Hackett, 2000), pp. 220–236. Eirik Harris also develops this idea in an interesting way in Eirik Harris, "The Role of Virtue in Xunzi's Political Philosophy," *Dao* 12(1): 108 (2013). Siufu Tang also supports a similar position in "*Xing* and Xunzi's Understanding of Our Nature," in Eric Hutton (ed.) *Dao Companion to the Philosophy of Xunzi* (Dordrecht: Springer, 2016), pp. 165–200.

32 See *Xunzi*, Ch. 1: 8.

3   Confucian virtue

> The Way lies in what is near, but people seek it in what is distant; one's task lies in what is easy, but people seek it in what is difficult. If everyone would treat their kin as kin, and their elders as elders, the world would be at peace.
>
> (*Mengzi* 4A11)

In the course of explaining why so many veterans long to return to combat, Sebastian Junger comments:

> What people miss presumably isn't danger or loss but the unity that these things often engender. There are obvious stresses on a person in a group, but there may be even greater stresses on a person in isolation, so during disasters there is a net gain in well-being. Most primates, including humans, are intensely social, and there are very few instances of lone primates surviving in the wild. A modern soldier returning from combat—or a survivor of Sarajevo—goes from the kind of close-knit group that humans evolved for, back into a society where most people work outside the home, children are educated by strangers, families are isolated from wider communities, and personal gain almost completely eclipses collective good. Even if he or she is part of a family, that is not the same as belonging to a group that shares resources and experiences almost everything collectively. Whatever the technological advances of modern society—and they're nearly miraculous—the individualized lifestyles that those technologies spawn seem to be deeply brutalizing to the human spirit.
>
> (Junger 2016: 93)

According to Junger, modern life, despite all its extraordinary technological and medical advancements, has created conditions ill-suited to satisfy the deepest yearnings of the human soul: a sense of purpose, belonging, and unity with those around us. We crave intimate connections and the shared pursuit of a common end, not more ease and comfort or sanitary lifestyles. According to Junger, it is the sense of oneness with those striving to achieve a shared goal that the veterans miss upon returning home.[1]

The need for rootedness and community is reiterated by the psychologist Alison Gopnik:

> Our local, particular connections to just one specific family, community, place, or tradition can seem irrational. Why stay in one town instead of chasing better opportunities? Why feel compelled to sacrifice your own well-being to care for your profoundly disabled child or fragile, dying grandparent, when you would never do the same for a stranger? And yet, psychologically and philosophically, those attachments are as central to human life as the individualist, rationalist, universalist values of classic Enlightenment utilitarianism. If the case for reason, science, humanism, and progress is really going to be convincing—if it's going to amount to more than preaching to the choir—it will have to speak to a wider spectrum of listeners, a more inclusive conception of flourishing, a broader palette of values.
>
> (Gopnik 2018)

Those of us in affluent nations have become increasingly attentive to the needs and suffering of those in less developed parts of the world; we are more aware than ever about structural injustices, global poverty, and violation of human rights. This is surely a good thing. But there is another aspect of morality, which seems to absorb the bulk of our everyday thought and energy, that consists in more local sources of concern such as carrying out the responsibilities we have toward our family, friends, and community.

At the heart of the Confucian moral tradition are virtues and goods directed toward building up flourishing intimate relationships and networks of human connections with a shared understanding of the common good. While the Confucian tradition does acknowledge certain impartial duties, on their conception the core of morality lies in our treatment and care of those most near and dear to us: our children, parents, spouse, or friends. Recall the inside-out direction of Confucian morality discussed earlier: our central ethical concerns center on our closest relationships and gradually spread outward. We can understand the Confucian virtues and goods as directed toward creating the sort of community and culture that Junger and Gopnik agree are necessary for good human lives. The study of Confucianism can help us achieve what Gopnik noted earlier as "a broader palette of values."

On the Confucian view, the development of good human relationships requires the development of virtues and the establishment of well-ordered families and communities. In the previous chapter, we saw that early Confucians posited the virtues as a constituent or basic component of well-being. This chapter aims to flesh out how these virtues are connected to well-being by showing how the Confucian virtues are oriented toward familial and communal flourishing. After first discussing the concept of virtue more generally, I will attend to the virtue of filial piety, a foundational virtue in the Confucian moral framework. We will also reflect on a core, distinctive feature of Confucian ethics, the notion of ritual (considered as both a virtue and a practice), which plays a pivotal role in the organization of families and communities.

The Confucian account of virtue

One trademark of Confucian ethics is its focus on the formation of good character rather than legal codes and harsh punishments. Consider Confucius's remark: "When it comes to hearing civil litigation, I am as good as anyone else. What is necessary, though, is to bring it about that there is no civil litigation at all" (*Analects* 12.13). While Confucius does not endorse the abolishment of legal regulations and punishments, he does not see them as the fundamental solution for creating good societies (*Analects* 2.3). A wise and effective teacher, for example, will not need to make heavy-handed use of punishments to keep young children in line but will employ less coercive strategies for bringing order to the classroom.[2] Confucius and his followers were focused on generating a deep and enduring change in the attitudes, desires, and emotions of the people. If their hearts could be turned toward the Way, then they would naturally follow the dictates of morality and act out of benevolence, and a transformation of the state would take place from within.

On this picture, the process of moral development runs deep, reshaping one's conception of what is good and worth pursuing:

> The Master said, "The gentleman cherishes virtue, whereas the petty person cherishes physical possessions. The gentleman thinks about punishments, whereas the petty person thinks about exemptions."
>
> (*Analects* 4.11)

> The Master said, "Eating plain foods and drinking water, having only your bent arm as a pillow—certainly there is joy to be found in this! Wealth and eminence attained improperly concern me no more than the floating clouds."
>
> (*Analects* 7.16)

We also find this prioritization of moral goodness over other external goods from Mencius:

> Mengzi said, "Fish is something I desire; bear's paw [an expensive delicacy] is also something I desire. If I cannot have both, I will forsake fish and select bear's paw. Life is something I desire; righteousness is also something I desire. If I cannot have both, I will forsake life and select righteousness. Life is something I desire, but there is something I desire more than life. Hence I will not do just anything to obtain it. Death is something I hate, but there is something I hate more than death. Hence, there are calamities I do not avoid."
>
> (*Mengzi* 6A10)

The early Confucian Xunzi, as noted in Chapter 1, also praises virtue's value over and above that of external goods, stating that the virtuous person loves virtue "more than the five colors" and "considers it more profitable than possessing the whole world" (*Xunzi*, Ch. 1: 8). As each of these early Confucians suggests, the virtues reconfigure our judgments about reasons for action in deep and systematic ways. As we grow in virtue, we revise our understanding of what is valuable or good. And the shift in priorities, as we see in these passages, is not trivial. Mencius claims a willingness to even die for the sake of righteousness, and Xunzi claims that the virtuous person values what is right more than possessing the world.

One significant point arising from this discussion is that the development of the virtues radically alters one's conception of well-being. On at least some subjectivist accounts of well-being, such as desire-satisfaction or value fulfillment theory, what constitutes one's well-being can change in the course of moral development if one's desires or values change. But on the early Confucian account, one's understanding of well-being can become more accurate by becoming more virtuous. The virtues help us achieve a clearer grasp of well-being by enabling the practice of virtue (e.g. ritual activity or filial acts) and honing our emotional capacity in ways that help reveal to us the real worth of objects. They also provide the proper epistemological perspective for understanding human flourishing.

It is also worth noting a distinction we might draw between virtues and virtuous activity. While virtues are good characteristic traits, virtuous activities are those activities that exercise those traits. Although engaging in virtuous activities, especially ritual practices, are central to the Confucian form of life, the virtues are also extremely important on the Confucian view because they refine our emotions, desires, and attitudes. The virtues bring with them a wholehearted commitment to following the Way. Both the virtues or good traits of character and the active engagement in practices such as ritual are also necessary for the flourishing Confucian life.

Many recent scholars who advocate a virtue ethical interpretation of the early Confucians have also endorsed some form of ethical particularism as best capturing the ethical reasoning of early Confucian thinkers.[3] Whether the early Confucians were particularists depends on how we understand that term of art. For while it is true that the early Confucians do not see moral principles as sufficient for living well, and do not see the paradigm of ethical reasoning as lying primarily in deducing right action through the application of certain principles, we do find the endorsement of certain absolute moral prohibitions in the early Confucians. For example, Mencius says, "if any [virtuous person] could obtain the world by performing one unrighteous deed, or killing one innocent person, he would not do it" (*Mengzi* 2A2.24). Similarly Xunzi claims, "Even if they [former sages] could obtain the whole world by performing a single act that goes against *yi* or by killing a single innocent person, they would not do it" (*Xunzi*, Ch. 8: 54–55).

While there is no clear decision procedure that the virtuous person applies to derive what ought to be done in any given situation from a set of moral principles, the passages just cited show that there are certain kinds of acts that are never permissible on the Confucian view. Of course, determining whether a certain situation involves that kind of action will require the right kind of moral perception. In describing the gentleman (*junzi* 君子), Xunzi states: "He fears troubles, but will not avoid dying when it is for the sake of what is *yi*. He desires what is beneficial, but will not do what he considers wrong" (*Xunzi*, Ch. 3: 17). The Confucian virtues can be understood as providing certain broad principles for action: one should never act against the virtues of righteousness, filial piety, benevolence, or ritual propriety. Of course, determining whether a certain act falls under the category of righteousness, filiality, benevolence, or ritual propriety cannot be done through some mechanical procedure and must factor in all the salient facts within a situation, which requires the cultivation of a proper character and proper moral perception.

While moral transformation must take place internally and requires serious effort and dedication on the part of the agent, early Confucians recognized the critical need for situational support to help correct wayward inclinations and strengthen an individual's disposition to do good. Human beings need a series of nudges and promptings even when they possess a healthy amount of self-motivation. The early Confucians paid considerable attention to how environments and external conditions could help bolster the likelihood of acting well and help provide the motivational push in critical moments.[4] So while the early Confucians can be understood as taking seriously the need to develop firm habits of feeling, thought, and action through the cultivation of robust virtues, they were also aware of both human imperfections as well as the sensitivity of situational influences that have been well documented by social psychologists. Below we will discuss

Confucian rituals, which play an important role in setting the proper social conditions for both the cultivation and maintenance of the virtues as well as assistance in good conduct during times of struggle.

When it comes to whether or not virtue or moral goodness is a constituent (or fundamental component) of well-being, there is rampant disagreement among contemporary moral philosophers. One worry is that different philosophers operate with very different senses of well-being and virtue. In this book I have understood the concept of well-being broadly, as closely connected to the concept of the good life, because the early Confucians themselves do not distinguish between these two concepts.

The concept of virtue is also fraught with challenges; not only are there undoubtedly different conceptions or accounts of virtue, but there may even be different concepts at play. And while I have spoken of 'virtue' or 'moral goodness' as if they are near equivalent terms, they are also importantly different concepts. In discussions of contemporary moral philosophy, moral goodness is often employed fairly narrowly, connected to how well one carries out certain obligations and duties toward others in relation to acts like aiding the needy, keeping one's promises, and not lying, stealing, or killing. One can also have a related conception of moral virtues as pertaining to those characteristic traits that dispose one to act in morally good ways within a narrow domain. Such virtues may be best conceived as "other-regarding." But on many classical accounts of virtues that we find in the ancient Greek or Chinese moral traditions, the virtues are those character traits that are constitutive of a flourishing life. On this broader picture of the virtues, justice and generosity are certainly virtues, but moderation, courage, self-respect, equanimity, and ritual propriety can all count as virtues as well. These latter traits will frequently involve actions or activities that are not necessarily connected to obligations toward others, but to what directly benefits oneself.

Once we conceptualize virtues broadly, it seems more plausible to think of them as closely tied to well-being. Without at least a certain level of self-respect or tranquility of mind, it is hard to see how a person's life can go well for her. And if one reflects on those ordinary, everyday experiences that substantially constitute our lives, it becomes clear how a host of 'ordinary virtues' play a critical role in how well our life will go. The early Confucians take virtues as important for everyday living and are not restricted to actions pertaining to the narrow domain of the 'moral.' Another way of thinking about this, which may be more accurate, is that the early Confucians have a more expansive conception of the moral domain.[5]

It is a difficult question whether every single virtuous action is always in the interest of the possessor. Justice, for example, can require someone to sacrifice almost everything one holds dear, including one's life. As some

Confucian texts demonstrate, the Confucians recognized that one might have to choose virtue over even one's own life, and they do not explicitly address how in those cases one is better off for doing what is virtuous. But in no passage in the early Confucian texts, as far as I am aware, do we ever get a description of the agent who acts virtuously as giving up her own good.[6] I think one reason for their view lies in the way that they thought the virtues systematically reordered one's priorities and outlook, which significantly alters the way a virtuous person sees her own well-being. On this view, the virtuous person sees any wrongdoing as contaminating the prudential value of whatever goods are preserved or gained to the point that it is never in her overall interest to do what is wrong.

A number of prominent scholars of early Confucianism have defended the view that the early Confucian moral tradition can be understood as a form of virtue ethics.[7] This view is not without its detractors, but even if it were inaccurate to consider early Confucianism as a form of virtue ethics, there is no doubt that the early Confucians were deeply concerned with the cultivation of certain desirable character traits that they believed were crucial for living well.[8] The Confucians believed that these virtues were essential for one's own well-being and the flourishing of the community. In this way, as I have argued, they endorse what I call "virtue perfectionism"—the view that virtue is a constituent or fundamental component of well-being.

Most virtue ethicists who take an account of flourishing or well-being as essential to an ethics of virtue believe that the virtues benefit the possessor; one of the central features of virtues is that they are constitutive of a flourishing life. While Confucians embrace this view, usually termed 'eudemonism,' their focus is not on the way that virtues directly benefit the possessor but the way that virtues are inextricably tied to the good of families and communities. We see throughout the Confucian tradition a focus on the good of the whole and the well-ordering of parts. Here is Xunzi: "For every kind of work and practice, if it is of benefit to good order, establish it. If it is of not benefit to good order, discard it. This is called making one's affairs conform to what is central" (*Xunzi*, Ch. 8: 56). Xunzi's central point, I believe, generalizes to all valuable activities, and can be applied to virtue as well. The virtues, on this view, help strengthen social order for the benefit of the community. We might characterize the idea in the following way:

> *Social requirement for virtue*: A characteristic trait is a virtue only if it sustains or develops the family, community or society.

The connection between virtue and one's own flourishing is indirect; it is because families, communities, or societies bear an internal connection to well-being that virtues are necessary for well-being. So while I understand the Confucians as taking virtues as constitutive of one's own flourishing, their role in human life is largely derived from their service to the good of families and communities. But because healthy families and communities, which must be structured around well-ordered relationships, are essential for individual flourishing, virtues are in this way closely connected to individual well-being.

On this account, one aspect of the Confucian virtues is that they are characteristic dispositions that are necessary for developing either good relationships or good communities. This directedness toward the realization of well-ordered communities and families provides the unifying principle underlying the Confucian virtues; we see that it is the flourishing of human relationships that serves as the focal point of Confucian virtue.

To illustrate the way that Confucian virtues are understood as traits that promote a healthy society, it will be helpful to look more carefully at some core Confucian virtues. I will discuss two in particular: filial piety (*xiao* 孝) and ritual propriety (*li* 禮). While there are other virtues—such as benevolence (*ren* 仁), loyalty (*xin* 信), harmony (和), or righteousness (義)—that are crucial to the Confucian tradition, *xiao* and *li* mark out two distinctive values that can contribute to the contemporary understanding of the virtues, highlighting certain goods that tend to get neglected in other philosophical traditions. We do not, for example, find these virtues in Aristotle, the most prominent figure in the Western virtue ethical tradition.[9]

There is another feature of the virtues that is significant for well-being, noted earlier, which is that the development of the virtues can reshape how one conceives of her own well-being; our character and values deeply influence how we think of human benefits and harms. In this way moral development can also reshape what we think is in our interests. The early Confucians conceive of moral development as the process by which we come to see more clearly what is truly in our interests, by being able to distinguish between what is really valuable and what is merely perceived to be valuable. It is only by developing the right kinds of desires, emotional dispositions, and attitudes that we can come to correctly understand what constitutes our well-being.

Filial piety as a virtue

A virtue is a characteristic trait that disposes a person to feel, perceive, think, judge, and act in ways that are proper to a particular situation. Drawing on the ideas of Martha Nussbaum, we may also understand virtues as what allows us to act correctly within certain fundamental spheres of human experience that human beings confront in the course of a normal human life.[10] For example, drawing upon Aristotle's list of virtues,

Nussbaum argues that courage is necessary for overcoming fear in those situations that involve possible harm; moderation is important for curbing excessive appetite for pleasure; and justice and generosity are needed to correctly distribute and share limited resources. Of course, when it comes to specific judgments pertaining to each of the virtues—what exactly it is that, say, justice or generosity demands of us—there will undoubtedly be substantive differences between our view and that of Aristotle's. Still, as Nussbaum demonstrates, Aristotle successfully identifies a number of cross-cultural human experiences and virtues that most of us will find remarkably familiar.

Nevertheless, from a Confucian point of view, Aristotle does not sufficiently address a feature of human life that profoundly influences our habits, thoughts, and values—those experiences forged within the familial environment. It is within the context of the family that our initial values are formed, where we grow by developing and exercising our emotional, moral, and intellectual capacities:

> A young person who is filial and respectful of his elders rarely becomes the kind of person who is inclined to defy his superiors. . . . "Once the roots are firmly established, the Way will grow." Might we not say that filial piety and respect for elders constitute the root of Goodness?
>
> (*Analects* 1.2)

Within this dynamic, complex social environment, we establish our first significant human relationships and develop our initial thoughts about how we should relate to others, as well as the norms and expectations that govern social behavior.

At the early stages of our lives, we are wholly dependent upon the care of our parents or other family caregivers for both physical and psychological needs. It is difficult to over-emphasize the sheer attention and energy required of parents in raising a child. From the Confucian perspective, these facts about the tremendous benefits we receive from our parents during the most vulnerable period of our lives are charged with normative significance.[11] Not only do children have a duty to look after parents in old age, but they must also carry out a three-year mourning period after their deaths (*Analects* 2.18), obey one's parents even when they are in the wrong (*Analects* 4.18), and "give [one's] parents no cause for anxiety other than the possibility that they might fall ill" (*Analects* 2.6).

So from the Confucian perspective, there is a sphere of human experience connected to the relationships and interactions that one develops with one's parents and a corresponding virtue, filial piety, that helps us to properly feel and behave in this domain of human life. Filial piety helps us to feel and express deference and concern for those who have nurtured and cared for us during the most vulnerable period of our lives. That filial piety involves not only certain types of outward behaviors but also certain inner feelings and emotions is an important reason why filial piety can count as a virtue, for to truly possess the virtue of filial piety one must be disposed to act out of certain kinds of motivations, namely, out of a genuine sense of gratitude, affection, and love:

> Ziyou asked about filial piety. The Master said, "Nowadays 'filial' means simply being able to provide one's parents with nourishment. But even dogs and horses are provided with nourishment. If you are not respectful, wherein lies the difference?"
>
> (*Analects* 2.7)

Of course, just as there are substantive disputes about what justice or courage calls for in particular situations, there will be considerable debate about what filial piety requires of us under various conditions. In a well-known passage, for example, Confucius considers it to be "upright" for sons to cover the misdeeds of their fathers (*Analects* 13.18). When Mencius is asked what Shun (a venerated sage king) would have done if his father had committed a murder, he replies:

> Shun looked at casting aside the whole world like casting aside a worn sandal. He would have secretly carried him to his back and fled, to live in the coastland, happy to the end of his days, joyfully forgetting the world.
>
> (*Mencius* 7A35.6)

We also see Mencius endorsing the decision by Shun to make his incapable and morally corrupt brother the prince of Youbi instead of appointing a more effective, benevolent ruler (*Mencius* 5A3). These passages can be troubling to modern readers because they seem to suggest that filial piety may involve a kind of nepotism that can require unjust behavior. There has been heated debate among scholars concerning whether the importance placed on filial piety by early Confucian philosophers leads to the praise and endorsement of certain actions that we ought to evaluate as morally corrupt.[12] These are complex issues requiring careful textual exegesis that cannot be carried out here. For our purposes, the main question is this: must accepting filial piety as a virtue require one to act immorally? I do not think so. For as defenders of any sensible virtue ethical view would insist, no virtue (at least in practice) can be detached from a well-developed capacity to reason practically, what Aristotle calls phronesis and what Mencius calls *zhi* (智), commonly translated as 'wisdom.'

In order to act well in any particular situation, we not only need the relevant virtue(s) but also the ability to correctly perceive the morally salient reasons that are relevant to the particular situation, to wisely weigh those reasons, and to make a judgment, all things considered. This capacity for well-formed moral judgment develops from the social interactions and feedback that we receive from our community that is initiated within the familial environment. Additionally, Provis (2013) draws attention to the way in which each member of society must learn certain "social scripts" that allows one to recognize and instantiate certain patterns of behavior that matches social expectation, thus rendering social interaction intelligible. This point is important for our discussion because the learning of such scripts is initiated within the context of the familial environment, thus providing an additional reason for taking the parent-child relationship seriously.

Still, one might find all this attention to the virtue of filial piety strange and misguided. While we should reciprocate the love and care our parents bestowed upon us, this is just a general application of the principle of reciprocity rather than some distinct moral domain. Why such preoccupation with filial obligations? This is a natural question, and it is worth probing just why filial piety is considered such a foundational virtue in Confucian culture. After all, it is also not clear how the virtue of filial piety contributes to the greater flourishing of the agent who possesses it.

Let me at this point try to provide some possible reasons on behalf of the early Confucian tradition. While these reasons are not explicitly stated in the Confucian texts, at least in the way that I articulate them below, I think they build on some core ideas found in the tradition and are at least consistent with it. To make sense of filial piety, we need to attend to the social requirement for virtue. The way that filial piety is supposed to work for the benefit of oneself is largely indirect; filial piety works for one's own advantage because it helps establish the sort of culture and community conducive to one's own well-being. There are three ways filial piety does this.

The first is centered on a motivational point. While parents are usually sufficiently motivated to take care of their own children because of their intense love for them, the same kind of motivation often does not exist in adult children toward their parents. Of course, there is usually some natural affection and love involved, but the motivation is not nearly as powerful as in the case of parents toward the children. What the emphasis on filial piety within a culture does is to strengthen the motivation adult children have toward the parents and to nudge them toward greater concern. This is socially important because as human beings begin reaching the later stages of their lives, they are in greater need of assistance, and it is characteristically the adult children who are best positioned to help take care of them due to their intimate personal history.

The second point draws on a broader need for shared public concern toward those who are dependent and vulnerable in society. While it might seem that a society taking tough measures to swiftly discard those who seem to create the most burden on people—the disabled or elderly, for example—would be stronger (such thought motivated the eugenics movement in the early 1900s), I propose that a society or culture that neglects such people tends to find it more difficult to develop and sustain important civic virtues such as civility and respect. Most importantly, there is a sense of cohesion that becomes ruptured when people are unwilling to provide assistance to those who are most desperately in need.

Here I should draw attention to the important work that feminist philosophers have done in addressing issues regarding relationships built around dependency and care, especially the mother-child relationship. Feminist philosophers have demonstrated how impoverished our moral reflections are without adequate reflections on the moral experience of both those who are dependent on another's care and those who provide such care.[13]

In caring for those who are most vulnerable and dependent, the people within a society collectively expresses a concern that is independent of any particular benefits that those individuals might bring. Such care helps demonstrate the simple recognition of another's basic needs that are anchored not in perceived contributions to the total utility, but simply in being a member of the human community. In effect, such concern expresses the idea that they matter to us independently of their ability to contribute in some quantifiable way.

Another reason care and respect toward the elderly is especially important is because we recognize that we too will find ourselves in their situation at some point, and that we will also become increasingly dependent on the care of others as our physical and mental powers decline. Because old age and mortality is a prospect often marked by great fear and anxiety, a culture that neglects the elderly may breed greater consternation about the end stages of one's life. A society that is deeply filial toward parents and elderly in general will help mitigate the anxiety that accompanies the aging process by ensuring that they won't be abandoned or cast aside by their own children or other members of society. Our need to feel appreciated and loved does not end after the earlier and middle stages of our lives.

The third way the virtue of filial piety is integral to a flourishing community or society is its structural connections to other significant traits or virtues, for example gratitude and benevolence. One of the sources of filial piety, as we noted, is the deep sense of gratitude we have developed from the recognition of the benefits that our parents have conferred on us during the most vulnerable stages of our lives. And gratitude has been shown to be an important prosocial trait that not only contributes to the flourishing of social relationships but also to the happiness of the person who is grateful (Frederickson 2004). Sustaining filial piety and the gratitude that accompanies it allows us not only to appreciate the very gift of life, but it also reminds us that the goods we have come to possess are not simply the products of our individual talent and effort, but are partially and necessarily the result of the good will of those who cared for us. A healthy practice for anybody who is tempted by the myth of the 'self-made person' is to think very hard about those very early years during which one was heavily dependent on the care of others.

Some contemporary scholars of Confucian thought have recently drawn attention to the possible ways in which filial piety or special attachments more broadly may actually generate certain moral conflicts and perhaps even steer us down the wrong moral path. The difficulty is that reasons of partiality may clash with reasons of impartiality or justice and a strong emphasis on filial piety might lead us to unjust actions. The cases involving Sage-King Shun, who must decide what to do as a king when his own father is convicted of murder, carry this kind of moral complexity. But this is a general difficulty applicable not only to virtue ethical theories but normative theories in general. And to think that an ethical theory can bypass such difficulties and always give a clear and definitive verdict for every moral situation seems to involve an underappreciation for the complex nature of the moral landscape.

We may now glean a few insights from the preceding discussion of filial piety:

1   *The moral significance of roles.* Filial piety is by its very nature a role-constituted virtue. That is to say, it requires the recognition that the kind of role one occupies has moral relevance for determining the proper way one ought to feel and act toward others. Whether one is interacting with a colleague, student, teacher, business partner, friend, child, spouse, or parent influences what kind of behaviors are impermissible, permissible, warranted, or fitting.

2   *The importance of the family.* A deeper understanding of filial piety helps us to strengthen our grasp of the enduring impact that one's familial environment has on just about every aspect of our psychological and behavioral tendencies.[14] This is an instance of a more general fact that external conditions play a powerful role in determining the kind of person one becomes. With the support of decades of psychological and sociological research at our disposal, we need to be more

attentive to the ways in which our social (including familial) environment influences our psychological and behavioral tendencies. Both our characters and actions are marked by situational sensitivity.

3   *The importance of gratitude in moral life.* For the early Confucians, one's need to express gratitude for the significant benefits received from one's parents is the cornerstone of filial piety. Genuine filial piety requires one to not only behave in certain ways but also to possess the proper emotion of gratitude toward one's parents. To put it differently, one must not only perform actions that are merely in accordance with gratitude but act from the motive of gratitude.

The significance placed on filial piety in Confucianism is closely tied to the roles, families, and gratitude developed and sustained within the Confucian form of life. A culture that prizes filial piety is one that takes seriously the value of one's parents, especially in a challenging and vulnerable period, by building on the proper gratitude one ought to have toward them. One instrumental role served is the satisfaction that parents who are looking after young children can have in realizing the reciprocal nature of the child-parent relationship. In a culture that prizes taking care of one's elderly parents in old age, parents will have some assurance that they will not be neglected by their children in the future. Now, perhaps this may sound too instrumental; after all, we should love our children unconditionally, and a good parent does not care for their children because of future perceived benefits. But on the other hand, it does seem that a culture in which one's elderly parents are simply discarded like an old rag or given insufficient attention and care may undermine our confidence in the broader value of families and perhaps human relationships. And certainly for those elderly parents, their well-being seems closely tied to the extent that their children visit them or seem to be genuine appreciative of them.

Perhaps more importantly, the care that parents hope to receive from their children in old age isn't centrally about material goods but about genuine affection, gratitude, and psychological connection. A recent study of relationships between aging parents and their adult children in the United States suggests that elderly parents want a balance between autonomy and connection. They do not seek to be smothered by their adult children but do appreciate the fact that their adult children are there for them and willing to come to their assistance if needed. In the study, many decried the overprotectiveness of their adult children (Spitze and Gallant). Such studies also reveal the complexity of relationships between aging parents and their children, which likely vary in some ways across cultures and are shaped by cultural norms and expectations.[15] Nevertheless, I think the fact that parents hope for appreciation and a genuine connection to their children (at least in healthy relationships) seems to be shared across culture and time.

Confucian ritual

It is widely acknowledged by philosophers, cognitive scientists, and psychologists that our everyday experience with the world is filtered through various schemas that enable us to interpret, categorize, and organize objects. Even the ordinary perception of mundane objects like pencils, chairs, kimchi, or babies are all understood and made intelligible to us through a background framework that allows us to make sense of them. As Richard Nisbett notes:

> Without our schemas, life would be, in William James's famous words, "a blooming, buzzing confusion." If we lacked schemas for weddings, funerals, or visits to the doctor—their tacit rules for how to behave in each of these situations—we would constantly be making a mess of things.
>
> (Nisbett 2015: 20)

Rituals, on the Confucian view, are part and parcel of the practical schema that allows us to live together in community. They offer contextualized patterns of speech and behavior that allow us to communicate to others certain emotions and attitudes that are vital to human relationships such as acknowledgement and respect. One simple ritualistic practice we find in both East and West is a greeting, which can obviously come in different forms: a bow, handshake, hug, or fist bump. These simple gestures provide a basic rule of conduct that two people within a particular culture can understand as a basic sign of recognition. But even simple gestures like these require a shared understanding of meaning, and the following of certain basic norms that are necessary for successful execution. For a handshake, this would include the strength of the grip, length of eye contact, the duration of the grasp, and the physical distance between the two parties.

But what exactly are rituals? Like any complex concept, it is difficult to offer a precise definition, but the following characterization by Benjamin Schwartz captures the basic Confucian understanding:

> [A]ll those "objective" prescriptions of behavior, whether involving rite, ceremony, manners, or general deportment, that bind human beings and the spirits together in a network of interacting roles within the family, within human society, and with the numinous realm beyond.
>
> (Schwartz 1985: 67)

As we can see, rituals on the Confucian view are broad, covering a variety of small and large moments and events in human life. We also see that rituals are not simply value-neutral patterns of what people actually do, but they carry prescriptive force and provide normative standards for behavior;

an act violating these norms without good reason can be the subject of criticism by those within the community.

To some contemporary Western readers, however, the very idea of ritual is marked by negative connotations—a set of rigid, dull, and monotonous activities bearing little connection to morality or the flourishing life. The early Confucian attitude toward rituals couldn't be more different. Confucius tells his disciple:

> Restraining yourself and returning to the rites constitutes *Goodness*. If for one day you managed to restrain yourself and return to the rites, in this way you could lead the entire world back to Goodness.
>
> (*Analects* 12.1)[16]

Xunzi takes ritual as crucial for peaceful order and survival, as well as the proper channeling of desires and emotions for greater fulfillment: "And so when ritual is at its most perfect, the requirements of inner dispositions and proper form are both completely fulfilled" (*Xunzi*, Ch. 19: 204).

On the Confucian view, rituals are the blueprint of culture and society, providing us the "cultural grammar" for making our way through socio-moral space (Li 2007). They help regulate our everyday social transactions by delimiting the boundaries of what is appropriate or fitting in particular contexts. Take the act of a handshake. As Herbert Fingarette notes, what appears to be a trivial and effortless 'ritual' activity requires not only cultural understanding but expresses in a subtle way mutual recognition of shared humanity (Fingarette 1972). By drawing attention to socially shared understandings of what constitutes respectful behavior, rituals not only assist in smoothing out social interactions by allowing us to avoid potential areas of social conflict but also amplify those values vital for healthy communities.

How exactly the rituals hone and strengthen one's emotional capacity is left open in the Confucian texts, but drawing upon the empirical work of Antonio Damasio's "somatic-marker hypothesis," Sarkissian (2010) offers an intriguing answer. The Confucian social rituals (along with other cultural exercises) help create in their practitioners "somatic markers" that allow one to spontaneously respond to various situations with the appropriate emotional attitude. By mastering a wide range of ritual practices—bearing in mind the broad range of activities that are covered by Confucian ritual—one's emotional repertoire is expanded and strengthened, allowing one to feel and behave according to the norms of Confucian conduct in a wide range of circumstances. Of course, no set of rituals can possibly prepare a person for all the novel moral situations that one may encounter. Confucius himself was well aware of the complexities that arise within the span of a normal human life, and he advocated broad cultural learning that would have included a variety of Confucian arts: music, archery, charioteering, calligraphy, and mathematics.[17] Diligent practice in these disciplines, the recitation of the classics, and active participation in the rituals would lead the avid learner to internalize Confucian values and achieve the kind of emotional and cognitive balance necessary for successfully meeting the diverse array of complex moral and social challenges that must be managed in the course of human life.

Rituals on the Confucian view are not mere conventions that have been invented arbitrarily. They rest on deeper, more enduring human emotions and needs:

> From where did ritual arise? I say: Humans are born having desires. When they have desires but do not get the objects of their desire, then they cannot but seek some means of satisfaction. If there is no measure or limit to their seeking, then they cannot help but struggle with each other. If they struggle with each other then there will be chaos, and if there is chaos, and so they established rituals and *yi* in order to divide things among people, to nurture their desires, and to satisfy their seeking. They caused desires never to exhaust material goods, and material goods never to be depleted by desires, so that the two support each other and prosper. This is how ritual arose.
>
> (*Xunzi*, Ch. 19: 211)

The rituals, as Xunzi emphasizes here, played a vital role in getting us out of social discord and chaos by modifying our desires to enable coordination with others to better satisfy our desires.

To develop a greater appreciation for how rituals serve human needs and desires, I want to turn to a contemporary psychological theory that has gained much prominence in recent decades known as the self-determination theory (SDT).[18] By examining this theory in conjunction with some of the significant features of ritual as outlined by Xunzi, I think we can gain a clearer understanding of how ritual can play a substantial role in advancing our well-being.

According to the two founders of this theory, Edward Deci and Richard Ryan, there are three innate psychological needs that human beings share across cultures, which they claim are necessary for psychological flourishing: autonomy, competence, and relatedness. What follows is a brief sketch of these needs.

Autonomy

Human beings desire to exhibit control and see themselves as the source of action. Autonomy is closely connected to self-integration and self-regulation because paradigmatic instances of autonomous actions require a well-integrated self that does not suffer from internal conflicts. An addict, for example, has decreased autonomy because there are conflicting desires and loss of control.

Competence

There is a natural desire for human beings to learn and grow and to get better at certain tasks and activities. We see infants and toddlers at a very early age finding satisfaction from learning how to manipulate objects with their hands and move through space. As both Plato and Aristotle noted, human beings have a natural sense of curiosity and wonder.

Relatedness

We are intensely social animals who have evolved to live in relatively small groups and in community. And there is massive empirical research supporting the view that strong relationships are more significant for psychological happiness than any other basic human good.

According to SDT, we must satisfy these needs if we are to achieve psychological happiness. Among the three, it is clearly the need for relatedness that is most tightly connected to Confucian rituals because Confucian rituals are by nature social. The simple everyday rituals of greetings (discussed earlier) and sharing meals provide practices of engaging in social intercourse in ways that communicate affection and respect. And because rituals also bear a close tie to roles of various kinds, they help shape basic norms and boundaries that can help foster healthy relationships, for example, between parents and children or teachers and students. Because so often there are discrepancies in authority and power in these relationships, it is important to have certain well-established rules, for example, with regard to matters of sex between teachers and students. Obviously, there can be unhealthy norms as well and rituals that reinforce bad values. But hierarchy, deference, and roles are simply part and parcel of social life and seem to be ineradicable features of human life.[19] Rather than dismissing them, we need to use the tools of human wisdom, culture, and science to carefully reflect on how they are given the best shape within the context of human life.[20] We need to carefully reflect on the possible good that hangs on these social roles or hierarchies while at the same time being genuinely open to the possibility of revision and change when they better serve our ends.

But what about competence and autonomy? It seems that competence can be gained through the mastery of rituals by developing a keen sense of how and when to perform certain acts, such as what kind of facial expression and bodily posture one should maintain. Autonomy, however, seems to be a value that is in conflict with ritual because rituals are about providing basic protocols and rules for behavior and are directed at the common good. Moreover, rituals are transmitted through culture and tradition, which one might think are in conflict with autonomy. In fact, the Confucian tradition clearly does not value autonomy in the way that modern liberal societies do. Here I think a lot hangs on just what autonomy amounts to, and I would argue that rituals can help give expression to the value of autonomy when understood properly.

In fact, within the SDT, autonomy is not conceived as metaphysical freedom to choose between one option or another but is anchored in the development of a self that is free from internal discord. Autonomous actions are experienced by an agent as self-endorsed, that one can stand behind as an expression of one's self-identity. Such actions are also driven by the powers and capacities of the individual: "Quite simply, the concept of autonomy is deeply linked to the problem of integration and the feelings of vitality and experiences of wholeness in functioning that accompany it" (Ryan and Deci 2017: 97). Moreover, Ryan and Deci are careful to note that autonomy does not conflict with the fact of human dependency:

> Individuals who are autonomous will also, to a significant degree, be dependent in important relationship and interdependent with relevant groups. Independence does not imply autonomy but, rather, implies being either separate and/or not reliant on others. Autonomy as volition is as relevant for females as for males, for Easterners as for Westerners, for collectivists as for individualists. It is a basic human issue.
>
> (Ryan and Deci 2017: 98)

Let me illustrate how a ritual can help develop one's autonomy as well as satisfy the innate needs of competence and relatedness by drawing on the movie *Menashe*.

Menashe is a recently widowed Orthodox Hasidic Jewish man with a ten-year-old son, struggling to find his place in his religious community. Throughout the movie he is portrayed as a *schlimazel*, someone who is prone to misfortune or accidents. Against Menashe's wishes, the head rabbi has refused to let his son live with him until he remarries. Menashe has a hard time making ends meet while working at a small supermarket, and he is seen by his brother-in-law as a failure. The culminating scene in the movie is a dinner at Menashe's shabby apartment to carry out the *yahrzeit*, a ritual that marks the one-year anniversary of the passing of a loved one. Although he burns the *kugel* (a Jewish baked casserole) and smokes up the house, he pleases the rabbi with his sincere effort and gains respect from the members of his community.

The ritual of *yahrzeit* offers a way for Menashe to exercise his autonomy. Although the basic steps of *yahrzeit* are dictated by tradition, Menashe insists on holding it in his cramped apartment through his own preparation. He buys the traditional candle along with a modest but fitting painting for the occasion, and finds a recipe for the *kugel* from his neighbor. While there are certain guidelines that he must follow for the *yahrzeit*, he creates a suitable plan for carrying out the ritual, working his way around limited financial resources and small living quarters.

The rabbi's appreciation and praise of Menashe's ceremonial dinner, consisting of badly burnt kugel, seemed to be the result of seeing the effort and dedication Menashe exerted in his preparing for this meal. And although we see pressure from others to hold the *yahrzeit* somewhere else (for example, in his wealthy brother-in-law's home), Menasche deeply desires and stands behind his commitment to hold the ceremony at his home. For Menasche, the occasion for an ancient Jewish ritual becomes an opportunity to demonstrate his commitment and abilities. In this ritual, we find Menashe's autonomy and competence both being exercised.

The ritual of *yahrzeit* also provides Menashe and the other members of his religious community an opportunity to celebrate together, patch up grievances, and express feelings of gratitude and respect. The ritual and its expressive power help bind the community. Such rituals, deeply embedded within every religious tradition, nurture and sustain the social fabric of communities.

Recall that according to Xunzi, rituals arose to satisfy the basic desires of humans. A central way that Xunzi believed rituals accomplished this was by providing a mode of expressing certain fundamental human emotions such as joy and sorrow:

> In every case, ritual begins in that which must be released, reaches full development in giving it proper form, and finishes in providing it satisfaction. And so when ritual is at its most perfect, the requirements of inner dispositions and proper form are both completely fulfilled. At its next best, the dispositions and outer form overcome one another in succession. Its lowest manner is to revert to the dispositions alone so as to subsume everything in this grand unity.
>
> (*Xunzi*, Ch. 19: 204)

Xunzi affirms that there are certain proper forms that our basic emotions or dispositions must take on if we are to achieve psychological fulfillment. Xunzi repeatedly notes how rituals provide a certain structure and unity to our emotional lives. The idea might be that by giving order to our emotions, rituals provide a way of gaining psychological unity. Consider his choice of metaphors: "Thus, the ink-line is the ultimate in straightness, the scale is the ultimate in balance, the compass and the carpenter's square the ultimate in circular and rectangular, and ritual is the ultimate in the human way" (*Xunzi*, Ch. 19: 205). Just as without a ruler or compass our lines will be crooked and irregular, without rituals our attempt to express various human emotions will also be disordered and unsatisfying.

A core theme underlying this book is the way that well-being is conceived as deeply social and relational on the Confucian view. The rituals strengthen our sense of the human good as transcending a narrow sense of self-interest by forging intimate bonds with others.[21] There is, as recent scholars have pointed out, a kind of "oneness" that is established through communal and ritual activity—a loosening of strict boundaries between ourselves and others, and gaining the sense that we are inextricably connected to others in a profound way. The next chapter will continue to explore this social and communal orientation of Confucianism by focusing on the way that families play a critical role in human life.

Notes

1 In his outstanding book *Oneness: East Asian Conceptions of Virtue, Happiness, and How We Are All Connected*, Philip J. Ivanhoe explains how much of the East Asian philosophical traditions see the human self as essentially connected to others.

2 I borrow this example from Joel Kupperman's "Tradition and Community: Formation of the Self," in Kwong-loi Shun and David B. Wong (eds.) *Confucian Ethics: A Comparative Study of Self, Autonomy, and Community* (New York: Cambridge University Press, 2004), p. 107.

3 See Van Norden (2007: 58–59) and Loy (2014: 288–289).

4 See Sarkissian (2010) and Slingerland (2011).

5 I thank Gina Lebkuecher for this point.

6 Even in those passages which suggest that the virtuous person would give up her life instead of doing what is vicious (e.g. *Mengzi* 6A10), the virtuous person is not described as giving up her own good. On my view, they would have claimed that because preserving one's virtuous character is a higher good than preserving one's life, dying in these extreme circumstances actually is what is better for oneself, as counterintuitive as that might sound.

7 On the topic of the relationship between Confucianism and virtue ethics, I have learned much from Eric Hutton's discussion in Hutton (2015), which reveals the complexity of the topic. Tiwald (2010) and Angle (2009) also provide helpful discussions.

8 Among the detractors we also find a range of interpretive positions with regard to Confucian ethics including (1) role ethics (Ames and Rosemont 2011), (2) consequentialism (Im 2010), (3) Kantianism (Lee 2013), (4) care ethics (Li 1994), and (5) sentimentalism (Liu 2003).

9 But Aristotle does talk a great deal about friendship, which can hold between members of a family. For an insightful comparative discussion of friendship and filial piety in Aristotle and early Confucianism, see Connolly (2012).

10 Nussbaum (1993).
11 I should note that Xunzi's account of filial piety is noticeably different from what we get in the *Analects of Mengzi*, taking filial piety as requiring a grounding in broader ethical considerations (e.g. *yi*). But when considering most influential ideas that shaped the Confucian understanding of filial piety, I believe that the passages that arise out of the *Analects* and *Mengzi* had the deepest, most enduring impact. In saying this, I do not mean that Xunzi's view of filial piety is philosophically less satisfying. I actually find Xunzi's account of filial piety quite appealing. Thanks to Eirik Harris for pushing me to consider Xunzi's view more deeply.
12 Liu (2003, 2007), Guo (2007), Fan (2008).
13 For discussions of maternal care see Ruddick (1989) and Held (2006). For discussions of human vulnerability and dependency, especially with regard to disability, see Kittay (1999) and Silvers *et al.* (1998).
14 This point will be explored more in the next chapter.
15 It seems likely, for example, that elderly parents in modern America would seek more autonomy and independence from their adult children than elderly parents living in early China.
16 Slingerland translates *ren* (仁) as 'goodness' which one might object to, perhaps claiming that 'humaneness' or 'benevolence' are better translations. Slingerland opts for the more amorphous 'goodness' because he sees *ren* as underspecified and identifying a fairly broad, overarching moral virtue. I am not entirely sure what is the best translation and will simply go with Slingerland here. I thank Tim Connolly for pushing me to reflect more on this.
17 *Analects* 1.6, 6.27.
18 The most comprehensive picture of SDT is presented in Ryan and Deci (2017).
19 Jonathan Haidt includes authority/subversion as one of the foundational values of morality, which he thinks cross-culturally applicable. See Haidt (2012).
20 For example, the norms with regard to husbands and wives have developed considerably within American society in the last 50 years, directed toward equality and partnership. This is at least partially due to the realization that women have historically been unjustly impeded from pursuing a wider range of significant goods, such as the fulfillment derived from professional work. This is one way that ethical reflection can help revise our conception of roles in ways that are conducive to human flourishing.
21 See Ivanhoe (2017) for an insightful inquiry into this topic.

4 Family and well-being

The ancients who wished to manifest their clear character to the world would first bring order to their states. Those who wished to bring order to their states would first regulate their families. Those who wished to regulate their families would first cultivate their personal lives.

(*The Great Learning*[1])

In my very own self, I am part of my family.

(D. H. Lawrence *Apocalype*)

As we observed in the last chapter, the Confucian virtues of filial piety (*xiao*) and ritual (*li*) are aimed at developing, sustaining, and strengthening relationships that are fundamental to human lives. Another distinctive feature of Confucianism is its strong emphasis on the good of families. On the Confucian view, families are not simply one kind of institution or social organization among others but play a fundamental role in human life. Here we might distinguish between two different ways in which Confucians understood families as fundamental. The first is that the flourishing of families serves as a fundamental end. On this view, one central aim everybody ought to strive for is the good of one's family. The reason for pursuing the familial good is direct and non-derivative: the flourishing of one's family is constitutive of one's own flourishing. Considerations of the good of one's family is an intelligible good and a basic source of practical reason.

The second way in which families are fundamental to human lives is that they provide an indispensable psychological foundation for moral values and the cultivation of virtues. There has been some support by contemporary moral psychologists for the view that there are basic, morally directed human emotions and inclinations. As discussed in the previous chapter, studies by Paul Bloom at the Yale Infant Cognition Center have supported the view that babies as young as five months have certain kinds of moral (or proto-moral) dispositions that provide an inchoate grasp of basic moral concepts like fairness or the wrongness of harm. Of course, the range of moral values that are developed can vary enormously depending on one's culture and education. This is precisely why early moral education is also heavily emphasized by the early Confucians for shaping who we become. Our familial context provides, as noted in the *Analects*, the "roots" out of which goodness grows (*Analects* 1.2)

Families can, of course, take on a variety of forms, and the sexist, patriarchal aspects of family structure endorsed by the early Confucians should be rejected.[2] Despite worthy criticisms, however, the Confucians were primarily focused on the parent-child relationships and the way families serve as the basic building blocks of society. They were certainly right in emphasizing the special role that families play in determining how well or badly our lives go for us—a point that has generally been neglected by contemporary philosophers working on well-being. It seems to me quite plausible that no complete account of well-being could neglect the critical role that families play in human flourishing. While this discussion can only serve as a starting point for a topic that merits much more sustained efforts, I think extracting some of those elements of the Confucian account of well-being will provide a solid basis for defending the importance of families in understanding well-being.

Because there is a variety of forms families can take, it is difficult to give a precise definition of family. As one example of this variation, there is a narrower sense, sometimes called the 'nuclear family,' which includes parents and their dependent children, and the notion of 'extended family,' which can include grandparents, aunts, uncles, cousins, and others living within the same household. While recognizing the variety of forms families can take, the focus in this chapter will be on the parent-child relationship within families because that was the primary focus of early Confucians.

The rest of this chapter aims to identify and develop two significant connections between the good of families and well-being: (1) familial roles partially constitute the self, and (2) families provide the psychological foundation for moral self-cultivation. Developing these two connections will provide some support for a thesis that Confucians would happily endorse:

> *Well-being familism*: Family is a basic prudential good, a fundamental component of well-being.

While I find well-being familism quite plausible, I'm not aware of any clear defenses of it within the contemporary philosophical literature on well-being. Take, for example, the following list of objective welfare goods by four prominent philosophers:

JOHN FINNIS: Life, knowledge, play, aesthetic experience, sociability (friendship), practical reasonableness, 'religion.'

GUY FLETCHER: Achievement, friendship, happiness, pleasure, self-respect, virtue.

MARK MURPHY: Life, knowledge, aesthetic experience, excellence in play and work, excellence in agency, inner peace, friendship and community, religion, happiness.

DEREK PARFIT: Moral goodness, rational activity, development of abilities, having children and being a good parent, knowledge, awareness of true beauty.[3]

Friendship appears on three of the lists, and while we could think of particular relationships within the family as some form of friendship, it is still distinct from the concept of family. Parfit identifies "having children and being a good parent" as a good, and this does seem to be an integral aspect of the Confucian account of family, but what still seems missing is the crucial element of filial piety emphasized by Confucians, which consists in the proper treatment of one's own parents. The family, conceived by Confucians as a basic welfare good, is constituted by the mutual flourishing of parents and children.

In the next section, I will first explain the Confucian view that family is constitutive of the self and identity and explore how these points are connected to human welfare. The key focus here will be on the significance of roles, particularly as children and parents, and how they deeply impress on our conception of who we are. As scholars agree, the Confucians understood the self as relational, and one of the basic features of the Confucian conception of self is that we are part of a family. Second, I will discuss how our values and the process of moral development more generally are significantly shaped by our lives within the family. By establishing these two ways that families influence our lives, I hope to support the view that family ought to be considered a basic welfare good.

The self and roles

The concept of the self or identity, while morally significant, is difficult to pin down. We should distinguish between the concept of self discussed by metaphysicians, which focuses on what makes someone numerically the same over time, and the more substantive, 'thicker' notion that moral philosophers tend to be concerned with. In this discussion, by 'the self' or 'identity' I mean to refer to the second sense.[4] Joel Kupperman provides one way of articulating this concept, calling it "self-as-collage," which holds that the self "can be viewed as layers that represent the absorption (or sometimes, rejection) of various influences at various stages of life, going back to early childhood" (Kupperman 2004: 117). On this view there are different, complex facets to the self which develop over time.

The self seems to bear some important connections to well-being, especially because well-being has to do with what is good *for* a subject. For there to be well-being at all, there surely needs to be a self to benefit.[5] Interestingly, discussions of the self have been relatively rare in contemporary discussions of well-being.[6] Below I want to explore the notion of the self, as envisioned by Confucians, because this way of thinking about the self helps make the Confucian view concerning the internal connection between well-being and family more plausible and also helps to provide an interesting way of developing our understanding of well-being by clarifying our understanding of the self.

This is certainly not the only way to think about what the self consists in, and I am not attempting to provide a decisive argument for thinking about the self in this way. The Confucian view does not identify every aspect of the self as such. But the Confucian conception of the self does focus on some important aspects that support the connection between well-being and family.

It may be helpful to highlight a core idea within the Confucian account of the self—its close connection to roles. Here we might identify a radical and moderate version of this view, each argued for in the recent literature on the Confucian tradition. On the radical version, the self is nothing but a set of roles. We find this version advocated most prominently by Roger Ames and Henry Rosemont:

> In this Confucian view of the moral life, we are not individuals in the discrete sense, but rather are transactional persons living—not "playing"—a multiplicity of roles that constitute who we are. . . . We are, in other words, the sum of the roles we live in consonance with our fellows, cognitively and affectively.
>
> (Ames and Rosemont 2011: 112)

The self on this view is wholly constituted by roles. There is no aspect of the self that stands apart from the roles that are occupied. While I think Ames and Rosemont have done illuminating work identifying important features of roles and their significance, there are a number of objections to their view that I find persuasive.[7]

One is that if roles completely exhaust what the self is, then there won't be any capacity to step back from the roles to criticize them. Given some of the oppressive features of roles that have been endorsed within the Confucian tradition, this seems quite problematic. Second, it seems that there are general virtues the early Confucians identify which are not role dependent. For example, in the *Analects* we see in a variety of contexts discussions of the overall virtue of goodness (*ren* 仁), which Confucius does not always discuss as indexed to a particular role. Mencius's discussion of the four sprouts and virtues (as discussed in Chapter 3) also seem to be more general features of human nature and does not depend on the particular roles we occupy (*Mengzi* 2A6).

Now, it could be that when it comes to exemplifying the various virtues, consideration of roles will be influential, but that doesn't require one to think that the virtues are completely dependent on roles. As noted earlier, it seems that an ethical framework in which there are certain general virtues or broader moral values that are independent of roles carries an important advantage by allowing moral criticisms of certain roles and providing a way of settling conflicts when role-based obligations clash.

The moderate version that connects the self and roles takes the self as significantly, albeit partially constituted by roles, and see roles as both substantial and necessary for self-development and flourishing. In my view this is philosophically more plausible, and my aim here is to clarify and provide support for this position.[8]

The Confucians understood roles as normatively significant, providing well-defined standards for good and bad actions:

> Duke Jing of Zi asked Confucius about governing.
> Confucius responded, "Let the lord be a true lord, the ministers true ministers, the fathers true fathers, and the sons true sons."
> The Duke replied, "Well put! Certainly if the lord is not a true lord, the ministers not true ministers, the fathers not true fathers, and the sons not true sons, even if there is sufficient grain, will I ever get to eat it?"
> (*Analects* 12.11)[9]

On the Confucian view there is a close connection between the fulfillment of one's roles and one's level of well-being. By connecting well-being to roles, we can gain a clearer sense of well-being by situating it in terms of how well or badly we fulfill the roles we inhabit. Judging from how seriously people take the major roles they occupy, it seems reasonable that our evaluations about how meaningful and successful our lives are bound up with our judgments about how well or badly we fulfill our most significant roles, such as the roles we inhabit in our relationships or professions.

Suppose I receive poor teaching evaluations. If I believed those evaluations were justified, I would feel some sense of failure as a teacher; and if I understood my role as a teacher to be constitutive of who I am, this would negatively affect my judgment about how well my life was going for me. On the other hand, success in our most significant roles seems to at least be a sign, at least, that our life is going well for us. It would be difficult to imagine someone who was successful in every role she deemed important—as a teacher, friend, spouse, parent, child, neighbor, citizen— but that nevertheless did not have a life high in well-being. One reason is that what is involved in fulfilling these complex roles well is a host of human goods that seem central to a flourishing life. For example, one must have knowledge (a basic prudential good) to be a good teacher, and being a good friend requires having certain good characteristics such as honesty, empathy, and some level of psychological stability in one's own life.

One objection might be that success in a role does not guarantee finding subjective fulfillment in that role. There are certainly jaded office workers who might be highly successful but are miserable in their work. Over time, roles can lose their importance to us, and we might find ourselves carrying on with them only out of a sense of duty. Realistically, however, it seems likely that one who saw no value in carrying out a role would not be able to fulfill it adequately. If one really no longer valued being a teacher, friend, or spouse, one's motivation to do well in those roles would be significantly diminished. Now, perhaps the motivation could come externally; for example, one might be concerned about being a good lawyer only because this will help bring about wealth or reputation. At least when it comes to one's professional roles, this is a psychological possibility, although I have doubts about whether such purely external motivations could be sustained in the long term.[10] But more importantly, when it comes to other roles such as being a friend, spouse, child, or parent, the proper fulfillment of those roles requires not only certain outward actions but also proper feeling, thoughts, and attitudes. Confucius stresses this point:

> The Master said, "Nowadays 'filial' means simply being able to provide one's parents with nourishment. But even dogs and horses are provided with nourishment. If you are not respectful, wherein lies the difference?"
>
> (*Analects* 2.7)

Elsewhere, Confucius remarks:

> "Sacrifice as if [they were] present" means that, when sacrificing to the spirits, you should comport yourself as if the spirits were present. . . . If I am not fully present at the sacrifice, it is as if I did not sacrifice at all.
>
> (*Analects* 3.12)

In other words, the proper fulfillment of one's role as a filial child or as a ritual practitioner requires a certain attitude or emotion, which will likely be lacking if one does not have appreciation for the role.

Because of the relational nature of roles in Confucianism, by taking roles as significantly constitutive of the self, the Confucians also take the self as constituted by relationships. Who we are on the Confucian view is inextricably connected to our relationships. I am this person's child and another's father, husband, student, teacher, or friend. In this way the fulfillment of the self requires the fulfillment of these roles, and the flourishing of the particular relationships we hold.[11] Alasdair MacIntyre captures some core features of this view:

> In many pre-modern, traditional societies it is through his or her membership in a variety of social groups that the individual identifies himself or herself and is identified by others. I am brother, cousin, and grandson, member of this household, that village, this tribe. These are not characteristics that belong to human beings accidentally, to be stripped away, in order to discover "the real me." They are part of my substance, defining partially at least and sometimes wholly my obligations and my duties. Individuals inherit a particular space within an interlocking set of social relationships; lacking that space, they are nobody or at best a stranger or an outcast. To know oneself as such a social person is however not to occupy a static and fixed position. It is to find oneself placed at a certain point on a journey with set goals; to move through life is to make progress—or to fail to make progress—toward a given end. Thus a completed and fulfilled life is an achievement and death is the point at which someone can be judged happy or unhappy.
>
> (MacIntyre 2007: 33–34)

Having well-defined roles provides some clear criteria of success for moving through life. As MacIntyre notes, the roles are not rigidly fixed because we move in and out of certain roles. A child can later become a parent and grandparent. A student can become the teacher.

Of the various relationships discussed within Confucianism, it is the parent-child relationship that is given primacy. Not only is there temporal priority involved, but relationships with one's parents, at least during the earlier stages of one's life, carry enduring influence on us. It is also, interestingly, among the few relationships that we enter that are simply given to us. At least when it comes to our biological parents, there is no choice involved, and the fact that two people are my biological parents remains a fact whether or not I choose to have an ongoing relationship with them.

Among the central reasons why the early Confucians believed we owed so much to our parents is that they were our caretakers for many years, and that we were completely dependent on them for meeting all of our needs.[12] This is not to say, of course, that parents never abandon their biological children or that there can't be terrible parents. Giving up one's child for adoption can also be the best thing to do under some circumstances.

Drawing on the aforementioned ideas, we might offer the following argument for why families are fundamentally or non-instrumentally good for us. The aforementioned points might be captured in the following argument:

1   The self is substantially constituted by characteristic roles.
2   A characteristic role we take on is being a member of a family.
3   So, the self is substantially constituted by familial roles.
4   Fulfillment of roles constitutive of the self is non-instrumentally good for us.
5   So, fulfilling our familial role is non-instrumentally good for us.

One immediate objection will be that those without a family can flourish or have a life high in well-being. At this point, it is important to get clear on the sense in which family is a fundamental prudential good and how this idea is related to well-being in a more general way. We might distinguish between the following two claims:

1   One will have a flourishing life (i.e. a life high in well-being) only if one possesses the good of family.
2   The good of family provides a basic, non-derivative prudential value for the subject who has it.

I suspect that many would find (2) more plausible than (1), especially because (1) seems to go against the widely held view that there are a range of ways to achieve a flourishing life. On this pluralistic view, even if (2) is true, one might flourish without a family. For example, we can imagine a monk who peacefully lives a solitary life in the mountains and feels a profound connection to nature. Many of us would think such a person has a flourishing human life.[13]

But Confucians would likely have endorsed (1), and it is worth reflecting on what reasons they might have offered. One possible response they may have given is that even those who choose to happily live in seclusion, like the solitary monk, must have spent considerable time within a particular family, at least during their childhood. As Confucius comments in criticizing his disciple Zai Wo,

A child is completely dependent upon the care of his parents for the first three years of his life—this is why the three-year mourning period is the common practice throughout the world. Did Zai Wo not receive three years of care from his parents?

(*Analects* 17.21)

During those early years (as well as later years in childhood), one's well-being is significantly determined by the quality of the family within which one is raised. Indeed, our evaluations about the quality of our childhood seems heavily dependent on the familial environment. And here I mean not only to identify the instrumental value of having good parents for psychological stability, which I will discuss shortly, but also the basic prudential value of being part of a loving family that seems integral to childhood.[14] A complete lack of being a part of a nurturing family throughout infancy, childhood, and adolescence seems to diminish the overall assessment of well-being when considering a person's life as a whole. For while it is true that an important part of being a child is being properly directed toward becoming a mature adult, all those years I spent as a child were also just as much a part of *my* life as those later years. Those early years matter from a prudential perspective.

Of course, it is possible that one can have a miserable childhood, grow up in an abusive family, but still thrive in later years.[15] And we might still plausibly say that such a person had a flourishing life overall, despite the terrible early stages. There is no precise way to determine when someone's life has met the threshold of a 'flourishing' or 'good' life. How well our life goes, whether under or above the threshold of flourishing, comes in degrees. But still, whether one's childhood went well or badly remains a relevant fact in assessing one's life as a whole.

So while I think that, strictly speaking, the view that family is a necessary good for a flourishing life is shown not to be true because of these and other possible counterexamples, it is also not as implausible as it might appear. When it comes to claims about the fundamental welfare goods, it is better to take them as claims that are characteristic of human life generally rather than claims that pertain to logical necessity. For example, that smoking is bad for us is rarely disputed despite the fact that we all know that there are heavy smokers who live to a ripe old age.[16] Moreover, I think that when we do bring in considerations about childhood well-being, (2)—the more modest claim that family is a good which provides a basic prudential value—is fairly well supported.

Now (2) is just the thesis of well-being familism, and in this section I tried to motivate it by drawing a substantive connection between the self and familial roles. Even if there are cases in which one might not conceive of oneself as a member of a family, almost all of us are, at some point, part of a family and are dependent on the family in crucial ways, as stressed by Confucius. Of course, our connection to family does not exhaust the host of meaningful relationships we can enjoy, such as friendship or relationships within a community. This is one way, I suspect, that someone's life can still rank high in well-being without being a part of a family—by having deep and meaningful relationships in other ways. But family ties also do seem to occupy a special space that is not reducible to either friendship or community, and they are a part of the characteristically human life.

There is another significant idea that we find in the Confucian tradition: children are an extension of their parents. We find this in the *Classic of Filial Piety*: 'One's body, hair, and skin are received from one's father and mother. Not to injure these is the beginning of filial piety" (Legge 1970: *Xiaojing*, Ch. 1). In a well-known passage we find Mencius asserting, "Among the three unfilial things, to have no posterity is the worst" (*Mengzi* 4A26). One reason why having no posterity is unfilial could be that the family line is not extended, thereby severing a connection that the grandparents can have to the world even after they have passed away. In the West we also find similar thoughts in William James: "our immediate family is a part of ourselves. Our father and mother, our wife and babes, are bone of our bone and flesh of our flesh. When they die, a part of our very selves is gone" (James 1890: 292). More recently, speaking in more contemporary terms, Niko Kolodny comments:

> Taken for what it is, the genetic relationship consists neither in a shared history of encounter, nor in a common personal situation. It consists instead in the fact that the child's creation was, and its biological life has been, later stages of a continuous biological process (i) that began as an episode in the biological life of the parent and (ii) that has been governed throughout, in part, by the parent's genetic code: or, less clinically, by the parent's principle of organization, or specific Aristotelian form. That is, I think the literal core of the thought that your genetic child is your flesh and blood.
>
> (Kolodny 2010: 70)

Bracketing difficult metaphysical questions, it seems like James and the Confucian tradition are identifying a point that resonates with many people at the psychological level—that we characteristically do take our parents or children as an extension of ourselves.

Family as psychological and moral foundation

While in the preceding section I tried to provide an argument for well-being familism by appealing to the constitutive role that families play in one's identity, in this section I want to explore another reason for thinking that families are deeply connected to human well-being by reflecting on their psychological and moral influences. While in the previous section my focus was more on the non-instrumental benefits of family, here my focus is more on the family's instrumental benefits. If the virtues are constitutive of well-being for the Confucians, as I discussed in the last chapter, and families play a crucial role in the development of virtues, then there will be a strong instrumental connection between family and well-being.

In discussing filial piety in the last chapter, I noted how, on the Confucian view, it is within the context of families that our initial values are formed, where we mature (or fail to mature) by developing and exercising our emotional, moral, and intellectual capacities. As Confucius's disciple Youzi says,

> A young person who is filial and respectful to his elders rarely become the kind of person who is inclined to defy his superiors. . . . "Once the roots are firmly established, the Way will grow." Might we not say that filial piety and respect for elders constitute the root of Goodness?
>
> (*Analects* 1.2)

The metaphor of root (*ben* 本) is worth reflecting on. Not only does Youzi indicate that filial piety and elderly respect are a central source for developing one's moral character because they help initiate moral development, but he also implies that they continue to be an important source of moral growth throughout one's life. This point is emphasized by Mencius:

> When people are young, they have affection for their parents. When they come to understand taking pleasure in beauty, they have affection for those who are young and beautiful. When they have a wife and children, then they have affection for their wife and children. . . . But people of great filiality, to the end of their lives, have affection for their parents.
>
> (*Mengzi* 5A1)

As we observed earlier, the Confucian emphasis on the critical role that families play is partially due to the fact that our initial ethical formation hinges on the values we absorb from all those years within the familial life from infancy onward. Mencius boldly claims: "If everyone would treat their parents as parents and their elders as elders, the world would be at peace" (*Mengzi* 4A11).

That a healthy psychological life depends on being raised in a nurturing environment by our parents (or by at least one devoted caretaker) has been well established within contemporary psychology. One prominent and widely accepted view introduced by John Bowlby, known as "attachment theory," claims that for at least the first two years of infants' lives they must be continuously and consistently nurtured by at least one parent (or primary caretaker) to satisfy a natural human need for security (Bowlby 1969). If a secure attachment of this kind is not established, there is a host of negative long-term consequences that tend to follow, such as greater rates of delinquency, reduced intelligence, increased aggression, and depression. A key idea of attachment theory is that parents provide a "secure base" that allows the infant to engage in free play and to develop a sense of self as valuable. These early childhood experiences have a formidable role in providing psychological stability and significantly influence our sense of worth.

While the Confucian thinkers did not possess the kind of empirically driven understanding that was provided over 2,000 years later by psychologists like John Bowlby, they certainly recognized the centrality of familial life and its impact on children.[17] The early Confucians focused especially on the way that families provide both the initial stages and 'roots' of moral formation. Interestingly, the Confucian view about psychological and moral development as anchored in the familial environment is also closely connected to a central normative view that lies at the heart of the Confucian tradition: the concept of partial or differentiated care.

Consider the following well-known passage from the *Mengzi* about the actions of the Sage-King Shun (a central moral exemplar in Confucianism):

> Mengzi's disciple Tao Ying asked, "When Shun was Son of Heaven and Gao Yao was his Minister of Crime, if the Blind Man [Shun's father] had murdered someone, what would they have done?" Mengzi said, "Gao Yao would simply have arrested him." Tao Ying asked, "So Shun would not have forbidden it?" Mengzi said, "How could Shun have forbidden it? Gao Yao had a sanction for his actions." Tao Ying asked, "So what would Shun have done?" Mengzi said, "Shun looked at casting aside the whole world like casting aside a worn sandal. He would have secretly carried him on his back and fled, to live in the coastland, happy to the end of his days, joyfully forgetting the world."
>
> (*Mengzi* 7A35)

There are two points commentators often note about this passage. The first is that Mencius does not allow Shun to simply obstruct the legal process to save his father—a move that would have been easy to make—thereby demonstrating recognition of his duties as a king to all his people. The second is that what is truly praiseworthy here is that Shun's commitment to his father was so deep that he was willing to abandon his kingship.

One of the central ideas found in the classical Confucian texts is what is often called the doctrine of partial or differentiated care, which Bryan Van Norden characterizes as

> the doctrine that one has agent-relative obligations toward, and should have greater emotional concern for, those who are bound to one by special relationships, such as those between ruler and minister, father and son, husband and wife, elder and younger brother, and between friends.
>
> (Van Norden 2007:115)

Mencius's defense of partial care is actually a response to a prominent rival moral tradition, known as Mohism, that advocated "impartial care" (*jian ai* 兼愛) for all.

In a widely discussed passage, Mencius asserts, "Heaven, in giving birth to things, causes them to have one source, but Yi Zhi [a Mohist] gives them two sources" (*Mengzi* 3A5). Mencius criticized the Mohists' doctrine of impartial care by claiming that it requires "two sources" as the basis of human morality. According to a prominent interpretive line advanced by David Nivison, the one root (or source) of Confucianism is constituted by the natural inclinations of the human heart, whereas for the Mohists (according to Mencius), a second root is constituted by principles or doctrines (*yan* 言).[18] In advocating for both 'roots,' Mencius believed the Mohists were allowing for a chasm between one's desires and motives and one's normative views about how things ought to be, which would lead to long-term damage to our ethical sensibilities.

Here we observe how, for the Confucians, normative views and accounts of human psychology were deeply intertwined. The partiality of concern for which Confucians advocated can be understood as substantially generated by their psychological observations about human motivation and development. As the early Confucians recognized, from the very beginning stages of our lives we are naturally geared toward partial attachments to our parents and family members. It is within the familial setting that our most intimate and enduring bonds are formed, and where we also absorb, for better or worse, much of our initial set of values and beliefs. And because as children we need consistent and focused love from parents, we naturally forge a deep concern for our parents. The familial environments also allow us to begin the lifelong process of moral self-cultivation, of refining and developing those moral inclinations (or "moral sprouts" as Mencius calls them) that over time can become full-fledged virtues. Central moral emotions such as compassion, respect, and gratitude begin to take shape in children's lives, and in ways that are not fully fleshed out within the early Confucian texts, they become bound up with the love children receive from family members and the filial affection that naturally arises.[19]

We can observe a deep contrast between the Confucian account of virtue acquisition and certain views of moral development, most notably that of Lawrence Kohlberg, which takes the end stage of moral development as the achievement of an impartial, justice-oriented perspective that we find in the works of philosophers such as Immanuel Kant and John Rawls.[20] While the Confucians also believed that there were stages to moral development, they did not see the achievement of a justice perspective as the ethical ideal. Rather, cultivating deep affection and care for one's parents and family and supporting them in old age were considered to be central marks of a truly exemplary person.[21]

But as discussed in the last chapter, the Confucians also recognized the need to expand our care to those outside of our immediate circle of family and friends. As stated in the *Analects*, "Everyone within the Four Seas is one's brother" (*Analects* 12.1). And in Mencius we find prominently the moral concept of extension (*tui* 推), which advocates extending one's moral inclinations (or sprouts) to situations involving those who might appear to be outside of one's circle of concern. This is what I called earlier the *inside-out* approach to morality: we begin by cultivating a good character through local concern for those we bear special relationships to, and we gradually extend that concern to those who are less personally attached to us.

Here we might capture the central points of this section with the following brief argument:

1   Families are an indispensable source of cultivating the virtues.
2   Virtues are a constituent of well-being.
3   So, families are instrumentally connected to well-being.

If the Confucians were right that our moral values and the process of moral development are heavily influenced by our families, then it also seems clear that the self, which is significantly constituted by our moral values, bears a close connection to the family. Because our sense of self arises with, and is causally influenced by, the formation of our basic values and conception of the good, self-formation is bound up with the familial environment. So even if one were to reject the view that the self is constituted by familial roles, one might still hold that there is a strong connection between the self and family. And given that the fulfillment of the self is a crucial part of achieving well-being, we must at least acknowledge that a deep connection holds between family and well-being.[22]

A significant feature of the Confucian position on well-being is that how well one's family or those that one cares about fare directly affects one's own well-being. In other words, one's own well-being is partially constituted by the well-being of others. This view might seem problematic to some philosophers. After all, why should whether or not someone else's life is going well affect how well my life is going? Perhaps, one might think, knowing that someone who is close to you is doing well or badly might be connected to your desires or pleasures in some way and so derivatively influences your well-being. But why would just the sheer fact that, say, your mother or daughter is doing well or badly *directly* affect your well-being? Can we make sense of this?

The Confucian answer lies in the idea the human beings are fundamentally relational, familial creatures. The early Confucians believed that this conception of human beings was supported by facts about human dependency. The most obvious kind of dependency is found in infancy and childhood, when we must rely on the support of parents or primary caretakers for continued existence as well as emotional, social, intellectual growth, and moral growth. But the fact is that throughout every stage of our lives, we are continuously dependent on a host of conditions if we are to fare well. We need continued support from family, friends, and colleagues if we are to truly flourish. Moreover, recent empirical work in psychology suggests an impressive range of ways that our behaviors, thoughts, and motivations are deeply influenced by myriad situational factors. The recognition of the pervasive influence that situational factors have has led Confucians to emphasize the need to craft the right sort of environment. Xunzi is especially insistent on the powerful effects of social environment:

> Now if you live alongside people who are not good, then what you hear will be trickery, deception, dishonesty, and fraud. What you see will be conduct that is dirty, arrogant, perverse, deviant, and greedy. Moreover, you will suffer punishment and execution, and you will not even realize it is upon you. That is due to what you rub up against. A saying goes, "If you do not know your son, observe his friends. If you do not know your lord, observe his companions." Everything depends on what you rub up against! Everything depends on what you rub up against!
>
> (*Xunzi*, Ch. 23: 257)

Xunzi's emphasis on the ways in which our peers and our social environment affect our thoughts and behaviors has been reinforced by contemporary research in psychology and sociology, which alongside Xunzi provides us with reasons for exerting greater effort into investigating what Daniel Haybron calls "human prudential ecology"—the kinds of social environments under which human beings flourish.[23] This is a topic that has attracted less attention within contemporary philosophy, perhaps because it runs contrary to a pervasive belief in modern liberal societies that Haybron calls *individualism*: the belief that "human beings tend to fare best when individuals have the greatest possible freedom to shape their lives according to their own priorities" (Haybron 2008: 255). The opposing view, *contextualism*, claims that we fare better in environments that, to some extent, nudge us toward certain goods and ways of living.

Confucianism unequivocally endorses *contextualism*. On the Confucian view, humans are social creatures, susceptible to a variety of social influences; our individual identities are significantly constituted by an interlocking set of relationships formed within the family and society, and therefore, what is beneficial and harmful to us is importantly constituted by the interests of those that come to inhabit our social domain. Because we are ineradicably social creatures, Confucian thinkers would have been puzzled by an attempt to understand individual well-being that is severed from inquiries into flourishing families and communities. In contrast, contemporary philosophers working on well-being have tended to ignore how the nature of human relationships and our social environments are related to human flourishing, because, at best, they are thought only to provide us with knowledge of the necessary empirical conditions for achieving well-being. But if the human self, as the early Confucians believed, is substantially constituted by those relationships which we come to establish during the course of our lives, then it may turn out that any satisfying account of well-being must explain the connections between well-being, family, and community.

Notes

1 Chan (1963: 86).
2 In *Justice, Gender, and the Family*, Susan Moller Okin offers incisive criticisms certain kinds of family structure while also defending the importance of families (Okin 1991). But as Erin Cline discusses, Okin seems to have an overly instrumentalized view of the family, as valuable mainly because of its capacity to further gender equality. On the Confucian view, the family is a special and necessary form of social institution that provide a nurturing, caring environment for children. See Cline (2015: 242–243).
3 This list is drawn from Fletcher (2016: 149).
4 An interesting question is in what way the two senses might be connected. For example, it might be that the thicker substantive account of the self helps to preserve metaphysical identity.
5 An interesting question arises for systems of thought that deny the existence of a self, as in Buddhism. There may be an interesting, though complicated, story to tell about how individual well-being can be intelligible within this framework, although this is outside of the scope of this book.
6 One exception is Haybron (2008).
7 See Cokelet (2016) for a nice discussion of these objections.

8 Some defenders of the moderate position include Nuyen (2007) and Wong (2004).

9 Many scholars advocate reading this passage in light of *Analects* 13.3, which implies that the fulfillment of roles is a crucial part of developing and sustaining harmony in the world.

10 There is empirical support at least for the view that external rewards can decrease a person's motivation to do a job well, otherwise known as the 'overjustification effect.' See Deci (1971) and Leper *et al.* (1973). These studies do not directly show that one cannot sustain long-term motivation through external rewards, but they do call into question how effective external rewards can be.

11 See *Mengzi* 3A4 for the 'five human relationships' that are central to the Confucian tradition.

12 Philip J. Ivanhoe makes a compelling case for taking this as the central justification for filial piety in Ivanhoe (2007).

13 We might also note that celibate members of religious communities, such as Catholic or Buddhist nuns, brothers, or priests might be thought to belong to a family in a more extended sense. They may belong to a convent, monastery, or parish in a way that they see themselves as a 'sister,' 'brother,' or 'father' within that community. I thank PJ Ivanhoe for this point.

14 This is a central point established by Cline (2015).

15 As noted earlier, Sage-King Shun is a prime example of this.

16 I thank PJ Ivanhoe for this point.

17 Erin Cline has also drawn some insightful connections between Bowlby's work and early Confucian thought in Cline (2015).

18 See David Nivison's "Two Roots or One?" in Bryan Van Norden (ed.) *The Ways of Confucianism: Investigations in Chinese Philosophy* (Chicago: Open Court, 1996). See also Wong (1989).

19 Of course, not all children will feel this affection, which could be due to neglect by the parents themselves. The Confucians tend toward maintaining the need for filial emotions even when the parents are failing to carry out their roles.

20 See Kohlberg (1981).

21 In this way, Confucian ethics bears some striking similarities to feminist ethics of care as endorsed by Carol Gilligan, Virginia Held, and Nel Noddings (which, notably, also criticize Kohlberg, Kant, and Rawls). This comparison is nicely captured by Li (1994). Besides taking intimate relationships as central to the moral life, care ethicists (like Confucians) also incline toward some form of moral particularism that takes situational features as having ethical priority over general principles.

22 There is a danger of promoting a kind of "family worship," looking only at ideal families and failing to recognize the numerous ways in which families can diminish an individual's well-being through oppression and domination. Family life also comes with a host of difficult challenges and struggles. I haven't reflected on this point as much as I could have because I wanted to bring out the possible *good* that families provide. Moreover, despite these legitimate concerns, given the way that human beings are generated, nurtured, and raised, we simply cannot view family as an eliminable feature of human life, one that is simply another obstacle to overcome.

23 Haybron (2008: 253–282).

5 Joy and equanimity
The happy sage

The Master said, "Without Goodness, one cannot remain constant in adversity and cannot enjoy enduring happiness."

(*Analects* 4.2)

[T]o practice the Way by oneself when one does not obtain one's goal; wealth and prestige are incapable of seducing him; poverty and low status are incapable of moving him; awe and military might cannot bend him—it is this that is called being a great man.

(*Mengzi* 3B2)

[The sage] follows his desires and embraces his feelings, but what he establishes on their basis is proper and ordered.

(*Xunzi*, Ch. 21: 232)

The previous two chapters discussed several core features of the Confucian account of well-being including virtue, family, and ritual. The Confucians understood these elements as basic components of a human life that goes well and were committed to a form of objectivism about well-being. But one challenge with well-being objectivism is that it seems to open the space for a possible gap between well-being and psychological fulfillment. After all, what if one simply does not care about these various Confucian goods? Where does happiness fit within the Confucian picture?[1]

My plan in this chapter is to discuss two important aspects of the Confucian account of well-being that will help clarify how subjective fulfillment or happiness enters into the Confucian picture.[2] Two central points are involved in doing this. The first point is to discuss the kind of happiness that the Confucians believed would arise from the sort of virtuous life they endorsed. For the early Confucians, the path toward virtue and sagehood would give rise to a deep form of satisfaction where both emotions and values would be integrated harmoniously. One kind of enduring mark of a virtuous life, the Confucians contend, is the possession of what I will call *ethical equanimity*: a stable and reliable source of interior peace and satisfaction gained through a reflective, true judgment that one's life is directed toward the good.[3] This is a state closely tied to the concept of joy (*le* 樂) we find in the early Confucian texts, which has been carefully analyzed by both Philip Ivanhoe and Kwong-loi Shun.[4] My understanding of ethical equanimity is developed out of Shun's account of "reflective equanimity," though I prefer the term 'ethical equanimity' because it highlights the centrality of ethical goodness. While this mental state is distinct from pleasure, there are elements such as peace of mind and composure that are indicative of both happiness and a broadly healthy psychology.

One of the advantages of taking ethical equanimity as central to well-being is that it harmonizes with the view that the prudential value or disvalue of pleasure or pain, as well as emotions more generally, cannot be determined without appealing to a broader ethical context and considerations of one's life as a whole. For example, certain negative emotions that are generally considered painful, such as grief or anger, do not always decrease one's well-being on this account; within certain contexts, such emotions are proper responses that actually enrich one's life as a whole.

The second point of this chapter is linked to the first point about the need to contextualize the prudential value or disvalue of emotions. The Confucian idea here is that we should conceptualize our life as a whole in terms of a developmental, teleological structure. The Confucians, as I will argue, affirm the need to see our lives as unfolding in distinct life stages in a way that is geared toward certain worthwhile ends, especially sagehood.[5]

In establishing this point, I will also be supporting one of the key ideas I noted in the Introduction, which I called 'well-being holism.' Our well-being or the prudential value of human emotions cannot be understood without contextualization and a broader ethical framework.

I do not aim to provide in this chapter a decisive argument for demonstrating why the Confucians were right about ethical equanimity or the need to see our lives as developmentally and teleologically ordered. What I do hope is to show how these ideas are appealing in their own right and can work together to help provide a satisfying account of the positive subjective feature of human lives.

Ethical equanimity

A concept that lies at the heart of the early Confucian view of psychological satisfaction or happiness is the notion of *le* (樂), often translated as 'joy.' While the state of *le* is characteristically marked by qualities such as pleasure, ease, harmony, and tranquility, the Confucians believed that it can only arise when one has genuinely embodied an ethical orientation in one's life.[6]

Consider how Mencius ties the development of virtue with pleasure, which he sees as embodied in one's physical body:

> If one delights [*le*] in them [the virtues] then they grow. If they grow, then how can they be stopped? If they cannot be stopped, then one does not notice one's feet dancing to them, one's hands swaying to them.
>
> (*Mengzi* 4A27.2)

> A gentleman regards the benevolence, righteousness, propriety, and wisdom that are based in his heart as his nature. These are clearly manifest in his life and demeanor. They fill his torso and extend through his four limbs. Though he says nothing, his four limbs express them.
>
> (*Mengzi* 7A21.4)

These passages emphasize the particular form of satisfaction and joy accompanying virtuous activities (and one's evaluative judgments about them) as well as their manifestation in the virtuous person's physical form. We can imagine a deep serenity conveyed in the virtuous person's countenance and bodily posture that is apt to be seen as the mark of an enduringly happy state, free of anxiety, and resting on a kind of composed surety about the direction of one's life: "the gentleman has a concern to the end of his life, but he does not have a morning's anxiety" (*Mengzi* 4B28.7). Although Mencius does not fully articulate the details of the virtuous person's mental state, he clearly understands joy and positive psychological states (embodied in one's physical form) as necessary concomitants of a good life.

By taking enjoyment as arising from virtuous activities, Mencius's view appears to connect with Aristotle's idea that pleasure necessarily follows from, and completes, virtuous activities. One significant difference, however, is that while Aristotle holds that we come to enjoy virtuous activities for their own sake because of the inculcation of moral habits embedded within our developed second nature (the nature that arises from the influences of education and culture), Mencius takes our untutored 'first nature' (consisting of innate, unacquired characteristic traits) as already partially constituted by moral desires, implying that the pleasures of a virtuous life would also be partly explained by the content of our basic 'first nature.'[7]

Xunzi, as discussed in Chapter 2, did not accept the existence of moral sprouts, although he believed a virtuous life would also offer a deep source of satisfaction. Consider the following description of the sage by Xunzi:

> One who is truly sublime is a perfected person. For the perfected person, what forcing oneself, what steeling oneself, what precariousness

is there? Thus, those who are murky understand only external manifestations, but those who are clear understand internal manifestations.
The sage follows his desires and embraces all his dispositions, and the
things dependent on these simply turn out well-ordered. What forcing
oneself, what steeling oneself, what precariousness is there? Thus, the
person of *ren* carries out the Way without striving, and the sage carries
out the Way without forcing himself. The person of *ren* [humaneness,
benevolence] ponders it with reverence, and the sage ponders it with
joy. This is the proper way to order one's heart.

(*Xunzi*, Ch. 21: 232)

The sage's life and actions are in synch with her values, desires, and emotions. Her actions are marked by 'nonstriving' (*wu jiang* 無彊)—a mode of
unforced, natural behavior—adorned with emotional fulfillment and joy.[8]

We can note two reasons underlying Xunzi's view that the morally per-
fected life is also the most psychologically fulfilling. First, human desires
tend to expand and multiply. Without deliberative effort and training, desires
become increasingly unruly, causing not only ruptures in social relationships but also steadily increasing personal frustration. For Xunzi, only by
transforming our character through rituals can our desires become con-
trolled so that we not only live according to the Way but also optimize
the satisfaction of our own desires. Recall a passage cited earlier in which
Xunzi explains the origins of ritual:

From what did ritual arise? I say: Humans are born having desires.
When they have desires but do not get the objects of their desire, then
they cannot but seek some means of satisfaction. If there is no measure
or limit to their seeking, then they cannot help but struggle with each
other.

(*Xunzi*, Ch. 19: 201)

Second, Xunzi takes the life of virtue and participation in the rituals as the
highest achievable good: "And so, learning comes to ritual and then stops,
for this is called the ultimate point in pursuit of the Way and virtue" (*Xunzi*,
Ch. 1: 5). Xunzi affirms that a life centered on the practice of rituals and
virtues will provide us with deeper and more profound sources of satisfaction and joy than alternative ways of living.

Despite certain disagreements between Mencius and Xunzi concerning
human nature and moral development (as discussed in earlier chapters),
we see that they both take the life of virtue as marked by a well-ordered
psychological life. Lying at the heart of their view (as well as Confucius's) is what I labeled earlier as ethical equanimity: a stable and enduring

psychological state marked by composure and harmony that arises from a true judgment that one's life is directed toward a life of virtue. Kwong-loi Shun provides a helpful account of ethical equanimity (though he calls this phenomenon "reflective equanimity"), which he describes as an "enduring state of mind that is grounded in a reflective stance." Shun explains:

> [R]eflective equanimity is based not just on a reflective awareness and affirmation of the significance of the ethical, but also on a total reshaping of oneself to embody this awareness and affirmation. As a result, one would follow the ethical without effort even at the expense of things of deep personal significance to oneself. Such a transformation involves a fundamental reshaping of one's outlook on life as well as one's whole mode of being, including not just thoughts, feelings, and actions, but also one's demeanor and posture. In this sense, the Confucian ideal of reflective equanimity may be described as a spiritual ideal, if the spiritual is understood in a way that is divorced from pietistic and devotional practices.[9]

We might think of this as a *morally structured existence* that takes ethical values and principles as having priority over other goods. This doesn't imply that someone with ethical equanimity never errs or shifts from the morally proper path, but that there is a deeply grounded moral commitment to always live according to an ethical standard and to undergo moral self-correction when necessary.[10] Furthermore, the idea here is not that one must constantly have the occurrent thought that "this is what the Way requires," but that one's overall commitment to living virtuously influences whether or not one chooses a certain course of action. Consider a devoted father who spends most of his days laying bricks. While carrying out his professional tasks during the day, he may have few thoughts about his family. But while bricklaying is what occupies his mind during the day, it is not his overarching end. The goal of providing for his family is what ultimately gives sense and purpose to the bricklaying. If pushed for an explanation of why he lays bricks, he would eventually cite providing for his family as one of the central reasons. Most of us work with at least some implicit account of what is most important in our lives, even though the more important principles and values may rarely be made explicit.

As Shun also notes, ethical equanimity provides the subject with an enduring sense of peace because she understands herself as committed to living according to the Way, which on the Confucian view provides the highest ethical ideal. Of course, such a commitment does not guarantee lesser goods such as wealth or honor. But because it is the life lived according to the Way that is valued as what is most important, the person with this ethical orientation will possess a substantial level of contentment even in imperfect circumstances. One might identify here a kind of moral joy firmly planted in one's heart which protects oneself from falling into the kind of deep frustration, malaise, or emptiness that are hallmarks of an unhappy life.

If we take ethical equanimity as constituting the core of the Confucian view of psychological happiness, we can see that certain ways of thinking of happiness are ruled out on this view. First, happiness cannot simply be pleasure, contentment, or satisfaction, because ethical equanimity requires certain beliefs about what kind of life one is living. There is a conceptual tie between happiness, on this view, and evaluation or assessment about whether one is living according to certain ethical standards. One cannot sustain ethical equanimity while believing that one's life is directed toward petty goods, or worse, immoral practices. Or one cannot conceptualize one's life as marked by wholehearted commitment to virtue because one has celebrity status or a private jet (absent an elaborate story). The ethical ideal that one is directed toward cannot simply be about *anything*: it must be about ethical considerations, pertaining to things like honesty, care, and integrity.[11]

Sustaining ethical equanimity requires affirming that one is striving to live as a person with integrity. This conception of oneself, I submit, would also engender a form of self-respect because the agent views herself as guided by her most important values. One possible worry here might be a kind of self-righteousness or moral overconfidence arising from this self-conception. But a crucial part of the Confucian program of moral development is the honest probing of oneself through critical self-examination:

> Everyday I examine myself on three counts: in my dealing with others, have I in any way failed to be dutiful? In my interactions with friends and associates, have I in any way failed to be trustworthy? Finally, have I in any way failed to repeatedly put into practice what I teach?
>
> (*Analects* 1.4)[12]

On the Confucian view, someone who is truly devoted to following the Way would be open-minded about discovering one's own shortcomings and be fully committed to working on moral improvement.

A different worry is that someone who is actually vicious might take herself to be upright and maintain ethical equanimity. While this is a conceptual possibility, once we really dig into psychological facts and inspect the biographies of those who were really vicious, I think we would see that such cases are extremely rare. Do those who participate in sex trafficking really see what they are doing as in line with what is good? A harder case might be someone from a warrior culture that takes burning up everyone in an enemy's village as what duty requires. Couldn't such a person have ethical equanimity despite the fact that he commits unspeakable atrocities? After all, the warrior sees himself as doing what is right and might even be an outstanding person within the parameters of his own community, taking care of children and the elderly with affection and care.[13]

But the Confucians understood ethical equanimity as not simply reducible to a certain outlook and feeling but attached to a genuinely virtuous life. Recall the earlier characterization of ethical equanimity as involving a reflective, *true* judgment about one's life being oriented toward the ethical path. On their view one cannot have ethical equanimity without actually having a life that is virtuous or at least moving toward virtue. Even if one believed carrying out genocide was what the Way required and believed herself to be wholeheartedly committed to virtue, she would still not have *ethical equanimity* because this requires *actually* moving toward virtue or being virtuous, which the vicious agent is not. Ethical equanimity, therefore, isn't simply a matter of one's internal perspective but requires hooking up to a moral reality in a proper way.[14]

The notion of ethical equanimity, as we find in the Confucian tradition, seems to challenge an assumption we sometimes find in the field of positive psychology, which is to take the value of positive emotion states and happiness as detachable from broader normative considerations. But this doesn't seem to chime with the way many of us (and certainly the Confucians) actually value positive emotions or happiness. Many, and I would submit most, do not think that positive feelings are always good for us. Hope or optimism, even when there is clearly no possibility of success, can be a sign of foolishness. Even gratitude, touted as one of the most significant positive emotions in recent years, might be misplaced or ungrounded. Usually positive emotions are bound up with some actual good, which is why ordinarily we do find them as contributing to our well-being.

On the other hand, it seems that certain negative emotions such as grief or anger can, within a certain context, be fitting and good. While much more needs to be said here, the Confucians understood emotions like grief as necessary for certain Confucian practices. Consider this description by Xunzi of someone carrying out a significant ritual for paying homage to the deceased:

> When the guests leave, the host sends them off and bows to them as they go, then returns and changes his clothing. He goes back to this position and cries, as if the deceased had left. How full of sorrow! How full of respect! One serves the dead as if one were serving the living, and one serves the departed as if one were serving a surviving person.

One gives a shape to that which is without physical substance and magnificently accomplishes proper form.

(*Xunzi*, Ch. 19: 217)

Sorrow clearly plays a necessary and vital role in carrying out this ritual. On the Confucian view, the value of positive emotions can only be understood by fitting them within a broader context.[15] On this view it is possible that even a negative emotion like grief can contribute to one's well-being. This might strike some readers as implausible, but consider the familiar analogy with a painting containing a patch of color that in isolation would be deemed as defective but which actually enhances the overall beauty of the painting. Similarly, it might be that grief can actually contribute to the overall prudential value of one's life, although in isolation it might appear to carry negative prudential value.

The Confucians would have taken the value of happiness or positive emotions as determined within the context of the ethical form of life they endorse. There are not, on this account, unqualifiedly good or bad emotions but emotions that are good or bad for us under certain situations. Furthermore, as discussed earlier, the Confucians believed that someone who is truly on the Way, with wholehearted commitment toward virtue, will sustain a stable form of interior joy that cannot be disrupted by the everyday irritations that gnaw at the best of us. It's not that the Confucian sage never feels irritated or is never in pain, but that the recognition that one is striving to live according to the most important principles provides a steady source of interior peace because one is continuing to live according to their conception of what really matters in life.

At this point I would like to turn to a final feature of the Confucian account of well-being that fits well with their holistic account of emotion and happiness, which I earlier referred to as the 'developmental structure of human life.' The Confucians believed that there was a developmental structure to our lives and that the achievement of well-being requires not only to see our lives as carrying out this structure but that it be oriented toward important, choiceworthy ends, especially sagehood. On this view, unless our lives are actually directed toward certain ends, we could not achieve well-being. A life that was misdirected in pursuit of trivial ends or simply drifted along with no purpose at all would not have been considered by the Confucians to be a life that went well.[16]

The developmental structure of human life

While a number of philosophers have claimed that the trajectory or the shape of one's life matters for well-being, their discussions have mostly focused on why a life that improves over time is higher in well-being than a life that declines over time.[17] David Velleman and Douglas Portmore have claimed that a life that goes uphill is better than one that goes downhill even if the sum total of happiness is equal in both lives just in case, and because an uphill life involves the redemption of earlier (bad) events in one's life, thereby adding overall meaning to one's life story. Both Mencius and Xunzi would probably have agreed with Velleman and Portmore about the significance of redemptive meaning, but I also think that they would have emphasized the teleological aspect of well-being, which takes seriously the idea that, in order for our lives to realize the kind of narrative meaning endorsed by Velleman and Portmore, they must be correctly oriented toward ends that have objective value. It is this trajectory toward a proper end (or ends) that provides the unifying thread necessary for narrative significance.

It is worth pausing here to reflect on the notions of 'meaning' or 'narrative significance' and how they are connected to well-being. It is difficult to give an account of these concepts, but we might explain them by drawing on a cluster of interconnected notions such as 'depth,' 'significance,' or 'importance.'[18] I think these notions cluster together because they capture a thought that I think most of us understand: certain events, experiences, or activities are more *meaningful* or *significant*. In short, they matter more than others. And while there is space in human life to at times relax and catch a silly movie on the plane, we can understand the idea that lives can be wasted on trivial pursuits. The Confucian thinkers were adamant that an adequate grasp of what is more or less important was itself a serious matter. Consider again the following passage of Mencius (discussed in Chapter 2):

> [I]f we want to examine whether someone is good or not, there is no other way than considering what they choose to nurture. They body has esteemed and lowly parts; it has great and petty parts. One does not harm the great parts for the sake of the petty parts. One does not harm the esteemed parts for the sake of the lowly parts. One who nurtures the petty parts becomes a petty person. One who nurtures the great parts becomes a great person. Suppose there is a gardener who abandons his mahogany tree but nurtures his date tree. Then he is a lowly gardener. One who unthinkingly ignores his back while taking care of his finger is a rabid wolf. . . . It is not the function of the ears and eyes to reflect, and they are misled by things. Things interact with other things and simply lead them along. But the function of the heart is to reflect. If it reflects, then it will get it. If it does not reflect, then it will not get it. This is what Heaven has given us. If one first takes one's stand on what is greater, then what is lesser will not be able to snatch it away.
>
> (*Mengzi* 6A14–15)

The distinction between a 'petty' and 'great' person is found throughout the early Confucian texts.[19] What can be clearly drawn from passages likes these is that Confucians think certain activities and lives are richer and more meaningful. Frequently they discuss these notions within the context of self-cultivation and virtue. Because virtuous activity, as discussed earlier, is a core feature of well-being for the early Confucians, it seems plausible that they would also have understood the categories of meaningfulness or depth as an element of well-being, although these connections are largely left implicit in the texts.

Let me return now to the discussion of the developmental, teleological structure of well-being. As explained in Chapter 3, both Mencius and Xunzi hold that the best human life culminates in sagehood; becoming a fully virtuous person is the proper end of all our strivings. But despite the fact that they disagree about the process of moral development through which we may attain this end, what they clearly accept is that there is a certain developmental trajectory that must be followed if we are to achieve flourishing lives. On their views, this trajectory takes its particular shape from the psychological, bodily, and environmental conditions that determine the rhythms and cycles of human life. Such conditions impose certain constraints on the structure of the process of self-cultivation. One point emphasized by both Mencius and Xunzi is that life unfolds through a series of stages, and that what unifies these stages is the continual progression toward virtue and sagehood; it is the movement toward virtue that provides flourishing lives with their narrative unity. The notion of life stages is significant and is embedded in the different metaphors invoked by our two Confucian thinkers.

Recall Mencius's agricultural metaphor for self-cultivation. A good farmer must work with those natural tendencies inherent within the seeds in order to provide them with the necessary care and attention for development. This requires that she understands the surrounding environment, for example, the salinity of the soil and the climate patterns of the region. Consider this brief parable told by Mencius,

> Don't be like the man from Song. Among the people of the state of Song there was a farmer who, concerned lest his sprouts not grow, pulled on them. Obliviously, he returned home and said to his family, "Today I am worn out. I helped the sprouts to grow." His son rushed and looked at them. The sprouts were withered.
>
> (*Mengzi* 2A2)

This parable draws attention to the importance of understanding the natural stages of development and why failing to understand the particular needs relative to each step can have disastrous consequences. (It also highlights the importance of patience in the practice of self-cultivation.) Just as the farmer must understand the natural sequence by which his sprouts tend to grow, we must also understand the sequence of development for the moral sprouts.

According to Mencius, our moral development also requires a long, slow and steady process, which takes those natural moral tendencies found in our nature and guides them toward virtue by providing the proper conditions for growth. Just like the maturation and growth of barley seeds, the development of our moral sprouts spans a number of distinct stages, ideally culminating in the achievement of a fully virtuous character. These stages of development are structured by the tendencies of our nature, so it is important to pay attention to the characteristic features of a particular stage of moral development because what is necessary for one stage may not be necessary for another.

Now recall Xunzi's employment of craft metaphors: the molding of clay into vessels, the carving of wood into utensils, and the sharpening of metal into blades. As noted earlier, these metaphors focus on the way in which our moral sensibilities are produced not out of the internal resources of our nature but by implantation through artifice and design. Nevertheless, even though Xunzi does not believe that there are natural stages of moral growth fixed by the moral sprouts of our nature, he still holds that there are certain steps to moral development that must occur for the achievement of sagehood. Reflect on the process of forging a blade. A blacksmith forging a metal blade begins by heating the metal at a high temperature, and then goes on to shape the metal on an anvil with a hammer. This is followed by the process of steady grinding to give the blade its sharpness, which is then followed by a further heating phase and brought to completion through a final stage of grinding. Xunzi believes that, in a similar way, moral development must occur in a step-by-step process, which begins with recitation of the *Classics* and introduction into rituals (*Xunzi* Ch. 1). Through study and repeated performances of ritual one's character begins to take on a determinate shape, and as it gradually becomes ordered toward righteous behavior, the agent continues to move forward to subsequent stages of moral development, ending in the achievement of sagehood.

So while Xunzi did not accept, as Mencius did, that our nature carved out the proper developmental path through which we can become fully virtuous, he did believe that our initial endowment and the process of cultivation through the correct rituals (a process discovered by the ancient sages) determined the sequence of development that must be traversed to reach the final end of the sagely life.

For both early Confucian philosophers, the achievement of well-being could not be separated from the teleological end (i.e. sagehood) that our lives ought to be directed toward; any evaluation of a person's well-being needed to be made in light of how well her life was moving toward her final end. This is why they would have rejected the idea that we can understand the prudential value of emotions or happiness without considering how they operate within the context of a life of virtue. We also find an outline of a Confucian stage-based narrative trajectory in Confucius's condensed spiritual autobiography:

> The Master said, "At fifteen, I set my mind upon learning; at thirty, I took my place in society; at forty, I became free of doubts; at fifty, I understood Heaven's Mandate; at sixty, my ear was attuned; and at seventy, I could follow my heart's desires without overstepping the bounds of propriety."
>
> (*Analects* 2.4)

We see that even the Master himself had to proceed through different moral stages over the course of at least 55 years. These reflections and others throughout the Confucian texts indicate that the early Confucians were less focused on what some philosophers call *synchronic well-being*, which concerns how well a life is going at any particular moment in time, but rather *diachronic well-being*, concerning one's life as a whole (or longer stretches of one's life). Moreover, they accepted the existence of norms that would regulate this developmental process, whether they were grounded in facts about our nature (Mencius) or culture (Xunzi). The weight that was attached to the success of one's life as a whole may explain why Confucian thinkers did not put as much effort into explicating what constitutes a person's good at a time—an issue central to most contemporary philosophical discussion of well-being. On their behalf, we could offer a tentative account of synchronic well-being that takes what constitutes a person's well-being at a time as the realization of those goods that help contribute to (or are constitutive of) the sagely life. But given their focus on the developmental stages of the flourishing life, they may have believed that offering a unified account of what ultimately constitutes a person's well-being at a time may not be possible, because on their views, what is good for a person at a time appears to depend on the particular life stage that one occupies. What is good for a developing child, they could claim, is significantly different from what is good for a mature, healthy adult, which is also importantly different from what is good for an elderly adult facing the final stage of her life.[20] Moreover, given the importance placed on roles within the Confucian tradition, it might also be that the temporal feature of roles (being a child or parent occurs at different temporal stages) makes it even more difficult to apply a single, clearly defined standard of well-being to any particular moment in a person's life.

Returning to the earlier discussions of ethical equanimity, a substantial part of the sustained joy that is constitutive of the Confucian form of life arises from taking oneself to always be moving toward the achievement of the highest end available to human beings (i.e. sagehood). Not only is a sense of integrity and self-respect generated by this path, but also a deep sense of purpose and meaning, which is plausibly considered as a necessary and crucial feature of well-being. In this way, the Confucians understood that an ethically grounded emotional state would yield a more enduring, stable form of interior harmony and joy. If the Confucians were right that the deepest aspects of our identity as humans consists in our power to live morally good lives, then it seems highly plausible that happiness cannot be separated from that substantial part of who we are; virtue and happiness are interconnected.

The early Confucians, as we have observed throughout this book, take a variety of elements of well-being such as meaning, virtue, and happiness as clustered together. A mind or heart that is fully at peace and fulfilled cannot be achieved, on their view, without becoming morally oriented toward objectively good ends; virtue or moral goodness provides the proper foundation for a harmonious and happy life. (Their primary argument for this claim lies in their account of the morally charged, socially oriented human psychology that we examined in Chapters 3 and 4.) This point is expressed in a well-known exchange between Mencius and King Hui of Liang:

> Mengzi had an audience with King Hui of Liang. The king was standing by the pond, gazing at the geese and deer, and said, "Do the worthy also delight in these things?"
>
> Mengzi replied, "Only the worthy delight in these things. Those who are not worthy, even if they have these things, do not delight in them. . . . The ancients were happy together with the people, hence they were able to be happy."
>
> (*Mengzi* 1A2)

The first point made by Mencius is that only the worthy or virtuous have the right frame of mind to truly delight in various goods. The second point is highlighted by the last line of this passage: *The ancients were happy together with the people, hence they were able to be happy.* The idea is that the ancients (here probably referring to the ancient kings) could find happiness only if their people also flourished, reiterating a central theme of this book: our individual well-being is closely bound up with the well-being of our families and communities. While this claim is not immune from counterexamples or arguments, it is anchored in deep facts about human beings and a certain conception of the self (explored in the previous chapter) that is highly attractive. It is a position built out of basic elements of human psychology and widely shared intuitive judgments about the way we are socially wired to fall or rise together—a point revealed by both the darkest and brightest moments in human history.

Notes

1 One worry raised along these lines by contemporary philosophers is known as the *alienation problem*, which Peter Railton characterizes in the following way: "It would be an intolerably alienated conception of someone's good to imagine that it might fail in any way to engage him" (Railton 2003). For other discussions of the alienation problem, see Rosati (1995, 1996).
2 The term 'happiness' is complex and can be construed in different ways. As I discuss it in this chapter, I mean for it to refer to a fairly broad concept that identifies an overall positive psychological state that engages one's desires and emotions.
3 Note that the characterization requires the judgment to be true, a point that will be discussed more fully later in the chapter.
4 See Ivanhoe (2011) and Shun (2014).
5 This point will be supported later in this chapter by drawing attention again to the agricultural and craft metaphors of Mencius and Xunzi, as well as Confucius's own spiritual autobiography. See *Analects* 2.4 and also *Analects* 16.7.
6 Throughout this chapter I am greatly indebted to the ideas of Kwong-loi Shun and Philip J. Ivanhoe for their discussion of *le* 樂 and the concept's close connection to ethical values.
7 Mencius's account of human nature was discussed in Chapter 2. Aristotle might have objected (as Xunzi also does) that the various moral sprouts Mencius identifies are not really *moral* because what is morally good can only exist within our culture, second nature. Here Mencius might have replied that these sprouts should still be considered moral because they have a certain kind of direction or trajectory. They aren't just neutral, content-less inclinations or desires that can simply develop in whatever direction. Consider our native linguistic capacity and our natural inclination toward acquiring language. It seems right to say that this inclination is *linguistic* even though language is learned through education and culture. Nevertheless, our basic linguistic inclination is not just any old inclination: they are geared *toward* language acquisition (even if they may never actually move in that way). Similarly the moral sprouts are naturally geared *toward* the virtues (even if they never go in that direction).
8 The text actually attributes *wu-wei* (無為) to the benevolent person and *wu-jiang* (無彊) to the sage. How exactly the benevolent person differs from the sage or *wu-wei* differs from *wu-jiang* is not entirely clear. My take is the sage always represents the perfect or ideal person and so perhaps is able to exemplify a higher form of *wu-wei* than the benevolent person.
9 Shun (2014: 143–144).
10 Justin Tiwald discusses a related concept which he calls "wholeheartedness" to describe a form of commitment that the Confucians had toward a life of virtue. I have learned much from Tiwald's insightful discussion of this notion. See Tiwald (2018: 179–183).
11 Philippa Foot also makes a similar point about the content restriction of what can count as morally good or bad. See Foot (1978).
12 Cf. *Analects* 5.27.

13 One might wonder to what extent someone like this truly believes what he is doing is right, rather than simply exercising his power. He might say in destroying the village, "Sure, mercy could have been shown, but we did not have an obligation to. This is just the way of the world."

14 One might worry at this point that even the horrifically deranged person can still enjoy all the benefits that come with ethical equanimity (even if he does not actually have ethical equanimity) by continuing to see himself as an upright person. What is interesting is that such a person must truly be devoted to living an ethically good life and is in reality failing to live up to his most cherished commitments (though he is not aware of this fact). So it still seems like this person has a tragic life and one that even he would deem an utter failure, were he to grasp all the moral facts.

15 Philippa Foot and Elizabeth Anscombe have done much work highlighting the way that emotions like pride (and moral judgments broadly) are given their sense within certain contexts. We cannot, for example, call any action (e.g. running around a tree) morally good or bad without a special background. Ultimately, on this picture, concepts cannot be successfully deployed without meeting certain conditions. I've also learned much from Gavin Lawrence's discussion of this topic in Lawrence (2018).

16 The hollowness of a pointless life is displayed by the character Will Freeman (played by Hugh Grant) in *About a Boy*, who lives a luxurious but purposeless life built around an inheritance. Later in the film he finds deeper happiness by developing intimate connections and coming to care about others.

17 See Glasgow (2013), Portmore (2007), and Velleman (2000) for accounts of what Glasgow calls the "shape-of-a-life phenomenon," that a life that goes better over time is better than one that declines, even if the total amount of enjoyment in both lives are equal. However, Feldman (2004) and Kahneman (2000) deny the existence of the phenomenon altogether.

18 For a discussion of Confucius and the concept of meaningfulness, see Joshua Seachris and Richard Kim, "Confucius and the Meaning of Life," in Stephen Leach and James Tartaglia (eds.) *The Meaning of Life and the Great Philosophers* (New York: Routledge, 2018), pp. 1–9.

19 See also *Xunzi* Ch. 4 and *Analects* 4.11, 4.16. Matthew Walker also discusses the idea of hierarchical ordering in Mencius in Walker (2013), describing Mencius's view as a "structured inclusivism" about flourishing.

20 This point is developed in Kauppinen (2008).

6 Conclusion

This book began by citing the dissatisfaction some contemporary philosophers have expressed with regard to current philosophical debates about theories of well-being. On their view, these debates have gained an interminable quality, despite the expansion of theories and increasing sophistication of the most prominent contenders. Driven in part by this impasse, some philosophers have turned toward integrating philosophy with empirical psychology, with an eye toward providing a more realistic, empirically grounded picture of human flourishing.

I have followed the spirit of this movement in providing a Confucian account of well-being. In developing this account, we attended to a variety of human goods that are often missing in contemporary Western discussions of well-being, such as filial piety, family, and ritual. The Confucian tradition, as I have tried to demonstrate, provides an important resource for studying both the nature of these goods and how they contribute to our well-being. Because Confucianism aims at supplying a vision of how whole human lives and communities should be structured, it can provide a more complex account of how these goods enter into the lives of human beings and how they are anchored in communal norms, traditions, and human psychology. The central Confucian goods we examined gain their proper role and significance by being situated within the overall context of a Confucian way of life, with its developmental structure directed toward sagehood (as discussed in Chapter 5).

In the beginning of the book, I proposed three key ideas that would emerge from our reflections on well-being: well-being holism (well-being is inseparable from other fundamental values like virtue), the relationality thesis (human beings thrive by developing strong social relationships), and well-being contextualism (physical and social environments deeply influence well-being). An overarching lesson we might draw from these discussions is that understanding human well-being cannot be achieved without looking at the overall context of human life, which is always embedded in a particular community and a concrete culture. As I have argued, we cannot understand the prudential value of human emotions without an adequate grasp of how these emotions are situated within a social context that is inextricably bound up with specific norms and values.

These various social and cultural influences do not, however, arise in a vacuum but are also tied to basic psychological, physical, and developmental facts anchored in our nature as human beings. For while we have observed that the values and ideas of the early Confucian thinkers do diverge from those we find in contemporary Western societies, nevertheless, it is my view that when it comes to much of the basic core values and commitments of the Confucian thinkers, we are able to grasp their prudential intelligibility.

A number of philosophers, most notably Charles Taylor, have argued that a chronic feature of modern life is a sense of malaise, characterized by "loss of meaning, the fading of horizons" arising from a breakdown of traditional, hierarchical order that "gave meaning to the world and to the activities of social life" (Taylor 1991: 3). What the older system provided us, according to Taylor, is a "horizon of significance"—a background of intelligibility necessary for imbuing our lives and activities with meaning. The Confucian conception of human flourishing, with its strong emphasis on a robust, teleological moral order that can only be achieved within the larger context of one's family and community, perhaps provides a way of avoiding the kind of modern malaise described by Taylor; it offers a way of giving one's life a purpose or direction, a background or horizon that is crucial for attaching meaning to one's life.

Bibliography

Alcoff, Linda Martin (2007) "Epistemologies of Ignorance: Three Types," in Shannon Sullivan and Nancy Tuana (eds.) *Race and Epistemologies of Ignorance*, Albany: State University of New York Press.

Alexandrova, Anna (2017) *A Philosophy for the Science of Well-Being*, New York: Oxford University Press.

Ames, Roger (1991) "The Mencian Conception of *Ren Xing*: Does It Mean 'Human Nature'?" in Henry Rosemont Jr. (ed.) *Chinese Texts and Philosophical Contexts: Essays Dedicated to Angus C. Graham*, La Salle, IL: Open Court, 143–175.

Ames, Roger T. and Henry Rosemont Jr. (2011) "Were the Early Confucians Virtuous?" in Chris Fraser, Dan Robins, and Timothy O'Leary (eds.) *Ethics in Early China: An Anthology*, Hong Kong: Hong Kong University Press.

Angle, Stephen C. (2009) "Defining 'Virtue Ethics' and Exploring Virtues in a Comparative Context," *Dao* 8(3): 297–304.

Angle, Stephen C., Kwame Anthony Appiah, Julian Baggini, Daniel Bell, Nicolas Berggruen, Mark Bevir, Joseph Chan, Carlos Fraenkel, Stephen Macedo. (2017) "In Defense of Hierarchy," *Aeon*, 22 March. Available at: https://aeon.co/essays/hierarchies-have-a-place-even-in-societies-built-on-equality/ (Accessed: 15 December 2019).

Annas, Julia (2005) "Virtue Ethics: What Kind of Naturalism?" in Stephen M. Gardiner (ed.) *Virtue Ethics, Old and New*, Ithaca: Cornell University Press, 11–29.

Anscombe, Elizabeth (1958) "Modern Moral Philosophy," *Philosophy* 33: 1–19.

Antony, Louise M. (2013) "'Human Nature' and Its Role in Feminist History," in Stephen M. Downes and Edouard Machery (eds.) *Arguing about Human Nature*, New York: Routledge.

Baril, Anne (2013) "The Role of Welfare in Eudaimonism," *Southern Journal of Philosophy* 51(4): 511–535.

Besser-Jones, Lorraine (2014) *Eudaimonic Ethics: The Philosophy and Psychology of Living Well*, New York: Routledge.

Bishop, Michael (2015) *The Good Life: Unifying the Philosophy and Psychology of Well-Being*, New York: Oxford University Press.

Bloom, Irene (1997) "Human Nature and Biological Nature in Mencius," *Philosophy East and West* 47(1): 21–32.

Bloom, Paul (2011) *How Pleasure Works: The New Science of Why We Like What We Like*, New York: W. W. Norton.

——— (2013) *Just Babies: The Origins of Good and Evil*, New York: Crown Publishing Group.

Bowlby, John (1969) *Attachment and Loss*, Vol. 1: *Attachment*, New York: Basic.

Bramble, Ben (2018) *The Passing of Temporal Well-Being*, New York: Routledge.

Carson, Thomas (2000) *Value and the Good Life*, Notre Dame, IN: University of Notre Dame Press.

Chan, Wing-Tsit (1963) *A Sourcebook in Chinese Philosophy*, Princeton: Princeton University Press.

Chong, Kim-chong (2007) *Early Confucian Ethics: Concepts and Arguments*, Chicago: Open Court.

Cline, Erin M. (2015) *Families of Virtue: Confucian and Western View on Childhood Development*, New York: Columbia University Press.

Cokelet, Brad (2016) "Confucianism, Buddhism, and Virtue Ethics," *European Journal for the Philosophy of Religion* 8(1): 187–214.

Colla, J., S. Buka, D. Carrington and J. M. Murphy (2006) "Depression and Modernization: A Cross-Cultural Study of Women," *Social Psychiatry and Psychiatric Epidemiology* 41(4), April: 271–279.

Connolly, Timothy (2012) "Friendship and Filial Piety: Relational Ethics in Aristotle and Early Confucianism," *Journal of Chinese Philosophy* 39(1): 71–88.

Cua, Antonio (1977) "The Conceptual Aspect of *Hsün Tzu*'s Philosophy of Human Nature," *Philosophy East and West* 27: 373–389.

De Bary, Wm. Theodore (1996) *The Trouble with Confucianism*, Cambridge, MA: Harvard University Press.

Deci, Edward (1971) "Effects of Externally Mediated Rewards on Intrinsic Motivation," *Journal of Personality and Social Psychology* 18(1): 105–115.

Defoort, Carine (2008) "The Profit That Does Not Profit: Paradoxes with 'Li' in Early Chinese Texts," *Asia Major* 21(1), Third Series: 153–181, Star Gazing, Firephasing, and Healing in China: Essays in Honor of Nathan Sivin.

Durant, Will and Ariel (1968) *The Lessons of History*, New York: Simon & Schuster.

Fan, Ruiping (2008) "Consanguinism, Corruption, and Humane Love: Remembering Why Confucian Morality Is Not Western Morality," *Dao* 7(1): 21–26.

Feldman, Fred (2004) *Pleasure and the Good Life: Concerning the Nature, Varieties, and Plausibility of Hedonism*, Oxford: Clarendon Press.

Fingarette, Herbert (1972) *Confucius: The Secular as Sacred*, New York: HarperCollins.

Flanagan, Owen (1993) *Varieties of Moral Personality: Ethics and Psychological Realism*, Cambridge, MA: Harvard University Press.

——— (2014) *Moral Sprouts and Natural Teleologies: 21st Century Moral Psychology Meets Classical Chinese Philosophy*, Milwaukee: Marquette University Press.

——— (2017) *The Geography of Morals: Varieties of Moral Possibility*, New York: Oxford University Press.

Flanagan, Owen and Robert Anthony Williams (2010) "What Does the Modularity of Morals Have to Do with Ethics? Four Moral Sprouts Plus or Minus a Few," *Topics in Cognitive Science* 2(3): 430–453.

Fletcher, Guy (2016) "Objective List Theories," in Guy Fletcher (ed.) *Routledge Handbook of Philosophy of Well-Being*, Oxford: Routledge.

Fodor, Jerry (1983) *Modularity of Mind*, Cambridge: MIT Press.

Foot, Philippa (1978) "Moral Beliefs," in Philippa Foot (ed.) *Virtues and Vices, Collected Papers*, Berkeley: University of California Press, 96–109.

Fraser, Chris (2013) "Happiness in Classical Confucianism: Xunzi," *Philosophical Topics* 41(1): 53–79.

——— (2016) *The Philosophy of the Mozi: The First Consequentialists*, New York: Columbia University Press.

Frederickson, Barbara L. (2004) "Gratitude, Like Other Positive Emotions, Broadens and Builds," in Robert A. Emmons and Michael E. McCullough (eds.) *The Psychology of Gratitude*, New York: Oxford University Press, 145–166.

Glasgow, Joshua (2013) "The Shape of a Life and the Value of Loss and Gain," *Philosophical Studies* 162(3): 665–682.

Goldin, Paul (1999) *Rituals of the Way: The Philosophy of Xunzi*, Chicago: Open Court.

Gopnik, Alison (2018) "When Truth and Reason Are No Longer Enough," *The Atlantic*, April, viewed 9 September 2019, <www.theatlantic.com/magazine/archive/2018/04/steven-pinker-enlightenment-now/554054/>.

Graham, Angus C. (1989) *Disputers of the Tao: Philosophical Argument in Ancient China*, Chicago: Open Court.

——— (1992) *Two Chinese Philosophers*, Chicago: Open Court.

——— (2002) "The Background of the Mengzian Theory of Human Nature," reprinted in Xiusheng Liu and Philip J. Ivanhoe (eds.) *Essays on the Moral Philosophy of Mengzi*, Indianapolis: Hackett Publishing.

Guo, Qiyong (2007) "Is Confucian Ethics a 'Consanguinism'?" *Dao* 6: 21–37.

Hadot, Pierre (1995) *Philosophy as a Way of Life*, Michael Chase, Trans., Oxford: Blackwell.

Haidt, Jonathan (2012) *The Righteous Mind: Why Good People Are Divided by Politics and Religion*, New York: Pantheon.

Haidt, Jonathan and Frederick Bjorklund (2008) "Social Intuitionists Answer Six Questions about Morality," in Walter Sinnott-Armstrong (ed.) *Moral Psychology*, Vol. 2: *The Cognitive Science of Morality*, Cambridge: MIT Press, 181–217.

Handler-Spitz, Rivi, Pauline C. Lee, and Haun Saussy, trans. (2016) *A Book to Burn and a Book to Keep (Hidden): Selected Writings*, New York: Columbia University Press.

Haybron, Daniel M. (2008) *The Pursuit of Unhappiness: The Elusive Psychology of Well-Being*, New York: Oxford University Press.

Heathwood, Christopher (2007) "The Reduction of Sensory Pleasure to Desire," *Philosophical Studies* 133(1): 23–44.

——— (2010) "Welfare," in John Skorupski (ed.) *Routledge Companion to Ethics*, New York: Routledge.

Held, Virginia (2006) *The Ethics of Care: Personal, Political, and Global*, Oxford: Oxford University Press.

Hidaka, Brandon (2012) "Depression as a Disease of Modernity," *Journal of Affective Disorders* 140: 205–214.

Hurka, Thomas (1993) *Perfectionism*, Oxford: Oxford University Press.

Hutton, Eric, trans. (2014) *Xunzi: The Complete Text*, Princeton: Princeton University Press.

────── (2015) "'On the Virtue Turn' and the Problem of Categorizing Chinese Thought," *Dao* 14(3): 331–353.

────── (2016) "Ethics in the Xunzi," in Eric Hutton (ed.) *Dao Companion to the Philosophy of Xunzi*, Dordrecht: Springer, 67–93.

Im, Manyul (2010) "Mencius as Consequentialist," in Chris Fraser, Timothy O'Leary, and Dan Robins (eds.) *Ethics in Early China*, Hong Kong: Hong Kong University Press.

Ivanhoe, Philip J. (1990) *Ethics in the Confucian Tradition: The Thought of Mencius and Wang Yangming*, Atlanta: Scholars Press.

────── (2002) "Whose Confucius? Which *Analects*?" in Bryan Van Norden (ed.) *Confucius and the Analects: New Essays*, New York: Oxford University Press, 119–133.

────── (2007) "Filial Piety as a Virtue," in Rebecca L. Walker and Philip J. Ivanhoe (eds.) *Working Virtue: Virtue Ethics and Contemporary Moral Problems*, New York: Oxford University Press, 297–312.

────── (2011) "Happiness in Early Chinese Thought," in Ilona Boniwell and Susan David (eds.) *Oxford Handbook of Happiness*, Oxford: Oxford University Press.

────── (2013) *Confucian Reflections: Ancient Wisdom for Modern Times*, New York: Routledge.

────── (2016) *Three Streams: Confucian Reflection on Learning and the Moral Heard-Mind in China, Korea, and Japan*, New York: Oxford.

────── (2017) *Oneness: East Asian Conceptions of Virtue, Happiness, and How We Are All Connected*, New York: Oxford University Press.

James, William (1890) *The Principles of Psychology*, Vol. 1, Cambridge, MA: Harvard University Press.

Jensen, Lionel (1997) *Manufacturing Confucianism*, Durham: Duke University Press.

Junger, Sebastian (2016) *Tribe: On Homecoming and Belonging*, New York: Hachette Book Group.

Kagan, Shelly (1994) "Me and My Life," *Proceedings of the Aristotelian Society* 94, New Series: 309–324.

Kahneman, Daniel (2000) "Evaluation by Moments: Past and Future," in Daniel Kahneman and Amos Tversky (eds.) *Choices, Values, and Frames*, New York: Russell Sage, 693–708.

────── (2011) *Thinking, Fast and Slow*, New York: Farrar, Straus and Giroux.

Kastrup, Marianne (2011) "Cultural Aspects of Depression as a Diagnostic Entity: Historical Perspective," *Medicographia* 33(2): 119–124.

Kauppinen, Antti (2008) "Working Hard and Kicking Back: The Case for Diachronic Perfectionism," *Journal of Ethics and Social Philosophy* (1): 1–10.

Keller, Simon (2009) "Welfare as Success," *Nous* 43(4): 656–683.

Kim, Myeong-Seok (2010) "What *Ceyin Zhi Xin* (Compassion/Familial Affection) Really Is," *Dao: A Journal of Comparative Philosophy* 9(4): 407–425.

Kim, Sungmoon (2014) "The Way to Become a Female Sage: Im Yunjidang's Confucian Feminism," *Journal of the History of Ideas* 75(3): 395–416.

Kim, Youngmin (2011) "Neo-Confucianism as Free-Floating Resource: Im Yunjidang and Kang Chŏngildang as Two Female Neo-Confucian Philosophers in Late Chosŏn," in Youngmin Kim and Michael J. Pettid (eds.) *Women and Confucianism in Chosŏn Korea*, Albany: State University of New York Press, 71–88.

Kinney, Anne Behnke, trans. and ed. (2014) *Exemplary Women of Early China: The Lienu zhuan of Liu Xiang*, New York: Columbia University Press.

Kittay, Eva F. (1999) *Love's Labor: Essays on Women, Equality, and Dependency*, New York: Routledge.

Kohlberg, Lawrence (1981) *Essays on Moral Development. Vol. 1: The Philosophy of Moral Development: Moral Stages and the Idea of Justice*, San Francisco: Harper & Row.

Kolodny, Niko (2010) "Which Relationships Justify Partiality? The Case of Parents and Children," *Philosophy and Public Affairs* 38(1).

Kraut, Richard (2007) *What Is Good and Why*, Cambridge, MA: Harvard University Press.

Kupperman, Joel J. (2004) "Tradition and Community in the Formation of Character and Self," in Kwong-loi Shun and David Wong (eds.) *Confucian Ethics: A Comparative Study of Self, Autonomy, and Community*, New York: Cambridge University Press.

Lau, D. C. (2000) "Theories of Human Nature in *Mencius* and *Xunzi*," reprinted in T. C. Kline III and Philip J. Ivanhoe (eds.) *Virtue, Nature, and Moral Agency in the Xunzi*, Indianapolis: Hackett.

Lawrence, Gavin (2018) "The Deep and the Shallow," in John Hacker-Wright (ed.) *Philippa Foot on Goodness and Virtue*, London: Palgrave Macmillan.

Lee, Ming-huei (2013) "Confucianism, Kant, and Virtue Ethics," in Stephen C. Angle and Michael Slote (eds.) *Virtue Ethics and Confucianism*, 47–55, New York: Routledge.

Lee, Pauline (2000) "Li Zhi and John Stuart Mill: A Confucian Feminist Critique of Liberal Feminism," in Chengyang Li (ed.) *The Sage and the Second Sex: Confucianism, Ethics, and Gender*, Chicago: Open Court.

——— (2013) *Li Zhi, Confucianism, and the Virtue of Desire*, Albany: State University of New York Press.

Legge, James, trans. (1970) *The Chinese Classics*, Vol. 4, Hong Kong: Hong Kong University Press, 352, reprint.

Leper, Mark R., David Greene, and Richard E. Nisbett (1973) "Undermining Children's Intrinsic Interest with Extrinsic Reward: A Test of the 'Overjustification' Hypothesis," *Journal of Personality and Social Psychology* 28(1): 129–137.

Li, Chengyang (1994) "The Confucian Concept of *Jen* and the Feminist Ethics of Care: A Comparative Study," *Hypatia* 9(1): 70–89.

——— (2000) *The Sage and the Second Sex: Confucianism, Ethics, and Gender*, Chicago: Open Court.

——— (2007) "*Li* as Cultural Grammar: On the Relation Between *Li* and *Ren* in Confucius' *Analects*," *Philosophy East and West* 57(3): 311–329.

Liu, Qingping (2003) "Filiality Versus Sociality and Individuality: On Confucianism as 'Consanguinism'," *Philosophy East and West* 53(2): 234–250.

——— (2007) "Filial Piety: The Root of Morality or the Source of Corruption?" *Dao* 6(1): 1–19.

Liu, Xiusheng (2003) *Mencius, Hume, and the Foundations of Ethics*, Burlington, VT: Ashgate.

Loy, Hui-chieh (2014) "Classical Confucianism as Virtue Ethics," in Stan Van Hofft and Nafsika Athanassoulis (eds.) *The Handbook of Virtue Ethics*, Durham: Acumen.

MacIntyre, Alasdair (2007) *After Virtue*, Notre Dame, IN: University of Notre Dame Press.

——— (2013) "On Having Survived the Academic Moral Philosophy of the Twentieth Century," in Fran O'Rourke (ed.) *What Happened in and to Moral Philosophy in the Twentieth Century?* Notre Dame, IN: University of Notre Dame Press, 17–34.

Mills, Charles (1997) *The Racial Contract*, Ithaca: Cornell University Press.

Munro, Donald J. (1996) "A Villain in the Xunzi," in Philip J. Ivanhoe (ed.) *Chinese Language, Thought and Culture: Nivison and His Critics*, La Salle, IL: Open Court, 193–201.

Nisbett, Richard E. (2015) *Mindware: Tools for Smart Thinking*, New York: Farrar, Straus and Giroux.

Nivison, David S. and Bryan Van Norden, eds. (1996) *The Ways of Confucianism: Investigations in Chinese Philosophy*, Chicago: Open Court.

Nussbaum, Martha (1993) "Non-Relative Virtues: An Aristotelian Approach," in M. Nussbaum and A. Sen (eds.) *The Quality of Life*, Oxford: Oxford University Press.

Nuyen, A. T. (2007) "Confucian Ethics as Role-Based Ethics," *International Philosophical Quarterly* 47(3): 315–328.

Okin, Susan Moller (1991) *Justice, Gender, and the Family*, New York: Basic.

Olberding, Amy (2011) *Moral Exemplars in the Analects: The Good Person Is That*, New York: Routledge.

Pang-White, Ann (2018) *The Confucian Four Books for Women: A New Translation of the Nü Sishu and the Commentary of Wang Xiang*, New York: Oxford University Press.

Parfit, Derek (1984) *Reasons and Persons*, Oxford: Clarendon Press.

Phillips, J., J. De Freitas, C. Mott, J. Gruber, and J. Knobe (2017) "True Happiness: The Role of Morality in the Folk Concept of Happiness," *Journal of Experimental Psychology* 146(2): 165–181.

Phillips, J., S. Nyholm, and S. Liao (2014) "The Good in Happiness," in *Oxford Studies in Experimental Philosophy*, Vol. 1, Oxford: Oxford University Press, 253–293.

Poe, Edgar Allan (1980) *The Unknown Poe: An Anthology of Fugitive Writings*, edited by Raymond Foye, San Francisco: City Light.

Portmore, Douglas (2007) "Welfare, Achievement, and Self-Sacrifice," *Journal of Ethics and Social Philosophy* 2(2): 1–29.

Provis, Christopher (2013) "Judgment, Virtue, and Social Practice," in Howar Harris, Gayathri Wijensinghe, and Stephen McKenzie (eds.) *The Heart of the Good Institution: Virtue Ethics as a Framework for Responsible Management*, Dordrecht: Springer, 47–58.

Railton, Peter (2003) "Facts and Values," in *Facts, Values, and Norms: Essays Toward a Morality of Consequence*, New York: Cambridge University Press.

Raphals, Lisa (1998) *Sharing the Light: Representations of Women and Virtue in Early China*, Albany: State University of New York Press.

Rawls, John (1999) *A Theory of Justice*, Revised Ed., Cambridge, MA: Harvard University Press.

Robins, Dan (2011) "The Warring States Concept of *Xing*," *Dao* 10(1): 31–51.

Rosati, Connie (1995) "Persons, Perspectives, and Full Information Accounts of the Good," *Ethics* 105(2): 296–325.

—— (1996) "Internalism and the Good for a Person," *Ethics* 106(2): 297–326.

Rosenlee, Li-Hsiang Lisa (2006) *Confucianism and Women: A Philosophical Interpretation*, Albany: State University of New York Press.

Ruddick, Sara (1989) "Maternal Thinking," in Joyce Trebilcot (ed.) *Mothering: Essays in Feminist Theory*, Totowa, NJ: Rowman and Allanheld, 213–230.

Russell, Daniel (2012) *Happiness for Humans*, Oxford: Oxford University Press.

Ryan, Richard M. and Edward L. Deci (2017) *Self-Determination Theory: Basic Psychological Needs in Motivation, Development, and Wellness*, New York: Guilford Press.

Sarkissian, Hagop (2010) "Minor Tweaks, Major Payoffs: The Problems and Promise of Situationism in Moral Philosophy," *Philosophers Imprint* 10(9): 1–15.

Schwartz, Benjamin (1985) *The World of Thought in Ancient China*, Cambridge, MA: Harvard University Press.

Seok, Bongrae (2008) "Mencius's Vertical Faculties and Moral Nativism," *Asian Philosophy* 18(1).

Silvers, Anita, David Wasserman, and Mary B. Mahowald (1998) *Disability, Difference, Discrimination: Perspectives on Justice in Bioethics and Public Policy*, Lanham, MD: Rowman & Littlefield.

Shun, Kwong-loi (1997) *Mencius and Early Chinese Thought*, Stanford: Stanford University Press.

—— (2014) "On Reflective Equanimity," in Chengyang Li and Peimin Ni (eds.) *Moral Cultivation and Confucian Character: Engaging Joel J. Kupperman*, Albany: State University of New York Press.

Slingerland, Edward (2003) *Confucius: Analects: With Selections from Traditional Commentaries*, Indianapolis: Hackett.

—— (2011) "The Situationist Critique and Early Confucian Virtue Ethics," *Ethics* 121(2): 390–419.

Solzhenitsyn, Alexander (1974) *The Gulag Archipelago, 1918–1956*, London: HarperCollins.

Sperber, Daniel (1994) "The Modularity of Thought and the Epidemiology of Representations." In L.A. Hirschfeld & S.A. Gelman (eds.), *Mapping the Mind: Domain Specificity in Cognition and Culture*, New York: Cambridge University Press, 39–67.

—— (2005) "Modularity and Relevance: How Can a Massively Modular Mind Be Flexible and Context-Sensitive?" in P. Carruthers, S. Laurence, and S. Stitch (eds.) *The Innate Mind: Structure and Contents*, New York: Oxford University Press, 53–68.

Sperber, Daniel and L. A. Hirschfeld (2004) "The Cognitive Foundations of Cultural Stability and Diversity," *Trends in Cognitive Science* 8: 40–46.

Spitze, Glenna and Mary P. Gallant (2004) "The Bitter with the Sweet," *Research on Aging* 26(4): 387–412.

Standaert, Nicolas (1999) "The Jesuits Did NOT Manufacture 'Confucianism'," *East Asian Science, Technology, and Medicine* 16: 115–132.

Sung, Winnie (2016) "Mencius and Xunzi on *Xing* (Human Nature)," *Philosophy Compass* 11(11): 632–641.

Swanton, Christine (2003) *Virtue Ethics: A Pluralistic View*, Oxford: Oxford University Press.

Tang, Siufu (2016) "*Xing* and Xunzi's Understanding of Our Nature," in Eric L. Hutton (ed.) *Dao Companion to the Philosophy of Xunzi*, Dordrecht: Springer, 165–200.

Taylor, Charles (1991) *The Ethics of Authenticity*, Cambridge, MA: Harvard University Press.

Tiberius, Valerie (2018) *Well-Being as Value Fulfillment*, New York: Oxford University Press.

Tiwald, Justin (2010) "Confucianism and Virtue Ethics: Still a Fledgling in Chinese and Comparative Philosophy," *Comparative Philosophy* 1(2): 55–63.

——— (2018) "Confucianism and Neo-Confucianism," in Nancy Snow (ed.) *The Oxford Handbook of Virtue*, New York: Oxford University Press, 171–189.

Tomasello, Michael (2009) *Why We Cooperate*, Cambridge: MIT Press.

Van Norden, Bryan W. (2007) *Virtue Ethics and Consequentialism in Early Chinese Philosophy*, New York: Cambridge University Press.

——— (2008) *Mengzi: With Selections from Traditional Commentaries*, Indianapolis: Hackett.

Velleman, David (2000) "Well-Being and Time," in *The Possibility of Practical Reason*, Oxford: Oxford University Press, 56–84.

Walker, Matthew (2013) "Structured Inclusivism about Human Flourishing: A Mengzian Formulation," in Stephen C. Angle and Michael Slote (eds.) *Virtue Ethics and Confucianism*, New York: Routledge, 94–102.

Williams, Bernard (1985) *Ethics and the Limits of Philosophy*, London: Fontana.

Wong, David (1989) "Universalism Versus Love with Distinctions: An Ancient Debate Revived," *Journal of Chinese Philosophy* 16: 251–272.

——— (2004) "Relational and Autonomous Selves," *Journal of Chinese Philosophy* 31(4): 419–432.

——— (2015) "Early Confucian Philosophy and the Development of Compassion," *Dao: A Journal of Comparative Philosophy* 14(2): 157–194.

Wright, Robert (2017) *Why Buddhism Is True*, New York: Simon and Schuster.

Zagzebski, Linda (2017) *Exemplarist Moral Theory*, New York: Oxford University Press.

Index

Note: Entries with an n reference notes.

For Product Safety Concerns and Information please contact our EU representative GPSR@taylorandfrancis.com Taylor & Francis Verlag GmbH, Kaufingerstraße 24, 80331 München, Germany

Batch number: 08153772

Printed by Printforce, the Netherlands